Trilithon

The Journal of the Ancient Order of Druids in America

Volume I

Summer Solstice, 2014

ISBN: 978-0692211564
ISBN-13: 069221156X

Words of wisdom can be found in at least three places

In the sound of rustling oak leaves
In the tranquil voice of the stream
And in the pages within

Table of Contents

Letter from the Editor

As I write this introduction, spring has only begun to surface here in southeastern Michigan. After a long, difficult winter for much of the United States, the promise of a returned spring and the turning of the wheel of the year brings new hope, new life, and promise of good things to come. Like the seed that was sown before the dark months of winter and is now sprouting forth, so, too, has Trilithon come to have its time in the sun. Welcome to the inaugural issue of *Trilithon: The Journal of the Ancient Order of Druids in America*. I am very excited to introduce this publication into the Druid community and to continue to develop more discussion and scholarship surrounding Revival Druidry as it manifests throughout AODA.

Like Revival Druidry, the topics in our inaugural issue are diverse and represent a range of perspectives and paths. Starting in our roots, we have two articles focusing on the druid revival, including "The Myth of Einigan" by John Michael Greer and a "Blast from the Past" feature from an original ninteenth-century document in its entirety, titled "Letters on Tellurism, Commonly Called Animal Magnetism." These articles represent some of the foundations upon which our tradition is based, and learning more about our roots can influence our practices and knowledge in critical ways. Moving into the core of daily practice, Sara Greer describes devotional practices in detail, providing information on various ways of engaging in devotional activity, tending shrines and altars, providing various offerings, and the question that stumps many of us— what to do with daily devotional practice when one travels. We also have two articles on the Sphere of Protection (SOP); Tracy Glomski provides a fascinating intergration of the sword into the SOP, drawing upon material from the middle ages. Our second article on the SOP, written by myself, examines the energetics and uses for the SOP from my own experience. From the realm of the natural world and the ovate path, Paul Angelini encourages us to go out and forage for our own wild foods and medicine and how this foraging practice can seamlessly align with the Earth Path in our curriculum. Dana Wiyninger's "A Local Ogham: Finding Your Area's Sacred Plants" connects natural practice with diviniation; while Daniel Cureton's "Working through the Animals: Intuitive Bone Divnitionation" explores bone divination within Druidry. Now that the readers have some Ogham and bone tools, we can turn to Lexie Devine's "Crane Bags and the Druid Revival: A Personal Journey" where she describes the Druid's crane bag as a working tool and shares the story of her three crane bags. As you can see from this list, this first issue is full of material representing the broad range of AODA Druidry, and I'm sure it will serve readers well as food for thought, suggestions for practice, and themes for meditaiton in the year to come.

I'd like to conclude with some acknowledgments. First, Sara and John Michael Greer are to be deeply thanked for planting the initial seeds and helping water them. Their support and guidance have been invaluable. Karen Fisher has been wonderful in her copyediting work and deserves the highest accolades. Thank you also to all of those who have submitted articles, worked through ceaseless revisions, and have contributed their voices to this issue. Paul Angelini provided guidance on the layout and formatting of the journal. I'd like to thank and acknowledge the inner teachers of our order and those who have walked the path of Revival Druidry before us. Finally, I'd like to thank the living earth, who provided the materials for this journal and upon whom we depend for all things.

Please feel free, in future issues, to write responses to articles or any other letters to the editor—you can contact me at trilithon@aoda.org.

Yours in the peace of the maple grove,
Dana Lynn Driscoll
Chief Editor and Druid Adept, AODA

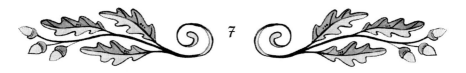

About the Ancient Order of Druids in America

Founded in 1912 as the American branch of the Ancient and Archaeological Order of Druids, AODA is a traditional Druid order rooted in the Druid Revival of the eighteenth and nineteenth centuries, offering an opportunity for modern people to experience the teachings and practices of Druidry in today's world. We don't claim direct descent from the original Druids—the priestly caste of ancient Britain, Ireland, and Gaul, which went extinct around 1,200 years ago—and to be honest, we're skeptical of any group that does make that claim. Instead, like other modern Druid groups, the AODA evolved out of a 300-year-old movement, the Druid Revival, that found the fragmentary legacy of the ancient Druids a powerful source of inspiration and insight, and drew on a wide range of sources in shaping a nature spirituality to meet the challenges of today.

AODA understands Druidry as a path of nature spirituality and inner transformation founded on personal experience rather than dogmatic belief. It welcomes men and women of all national origins, cultural and linguistic backgrounds, and affiliations with other Druidic and spiritual traditions. Ecological awareness and commitment to an Earth-honoring lifestyle, celebration of the cycles of nature through seasonal ritual, and personal development through meditation and other spiritual exercises form the core of its work, and involvement in the arts, healing practices, and traditional esoteric studies are among its applications and expressions.

Its roots in the Druid Revival give the AODA certain features in common with esoteric societies such as the Hermetic Order of the Golden Dawn. It offers an initial ceremony of reception into the order, followed by three degrees of initiation—Druid Apprentice, Druid Companion, and Druid Adept—which are conferred upon completion of a graded study program. Its members have the opportunity to meet in local groups of two kinds, study groups and groves, and a Grand Grove oversees the order, charters study groups and groves, and manages the study program.

In keeping with the traditions of Revival Druidry, the AODA encourages its members to pursue their own spiritual directions within a broad common framework, and its approach to spirituality is personal and experiential rather than dogmatic. The initiation rituals and study program are prescribed, and AODA members are expected to keep four traditional Druid holy days, the solstices and equinoxes. Creativity and the quest for personal Awen—the inner light of inspiration—are among the AODA's central values.

The Gnostic Celtic Church (GCC) is an independent sacramental church of nature spirituality affiliated with the Ancient Order of Druids in America (AODA), a contemporary Druid order. Like many other alternative spiritual groups in American society, AODA—which was originally founded in 1912—developed connections with a variety of other compatible traditions over the course of its history. One of these connections was with the Universal Gnostic Church (UGC).

For more information about the AODA's study program, please visit:
http://aoda.org/curric.html

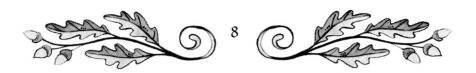

How to Join the AODA

The Ancient Order of Druids in America welcomes applications for membership from men and women of all spiritual, cultural, and ethnic backgrounds, age eighteen or older, who wish to create and follow a personal path of nature spirituality in the traditions of the Druid Revival.

By Mail: Send a letter of application to AODA, PO Box 996, Cumberland MD 21501 USA. The letter should include your legal name, Druid name (if you have one), postal and email addresses, date of birth, an outline of your previous Druid studies if any, and anything you may want to say about why you wish to join AODA and what you hope to get out of it. Include a check or money order for US$50, payable to AODA.

Electronically: Please send a letter of application via email to info@aoda.org. The email should include your legal name, Druid name (if you have one), postal and email addresses, date of birth, an outline of your previous Druid studies if any, and anything you may want to say about why you wish to join AODA and what you hope to get out of it. Your membership fee of US$50 may be paid via PayPal; please have payment made to payment@aoda.org.

How to Contact the AODA

Trilithon Journal
Contact the editor, Dana Lynn Driscoll, at trilithon@aoda.org

Contact the AODA
Contact the AODA Grand Grove at info@aoda.org

Mailing address:
AODA
PO Box 996
Cumberland, MD 21501

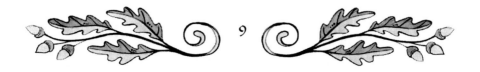

Finding the Awen in Field and Forest: Foraging and the Earth Path in the AODA Tradition

Paul Angelini

Paul Angelini is a native Michigander, avid wild food and medicine forager, and candidate for apprenticeship in the AODA. He has been a student of the natural world since his early youth, spending many hours in forests, swamps, and fields, basking in the beauty and splendor of nature. After being introduced to the masterful books of expert forager Samuel Thayer in 2011, he became fully committed to the art, and later began embarking on thrilling foraging adventures with his best friend and fellow Druid, Dana, notably trekking through a knee-deep bog in hunt of wild blueberries. Aside from being a forager, Paul is an aspiring herbalist, having completed a four-season herbalism intensive with noted Michigan herbalist Jim McDonald (www.herbcraft.org). His other passions include sustainability/appropriate tech, gardening, used book stores, local foods and businesses, farmers' markets, esoterica, and homebrewing and cyder-making. He also enjoys concocting craft cocktail syrups and bitters for his small startup company, Soda & Sundries (www.sodaandsundries.com).

Looking back just a few generations, we find that the ability to safely and correctly identify wild herbs, flowers, fruit, and so on was not just a matter of pleasure and convenience—it was what put food on the table and provided the medicine that helped us regain health. We may have heard stories of Great Grandma's wild raspberry jam on homemade buttered biscuits or the elderberry syrup she used to give Grandma as a kid when she was sick. The roots of this practice, or art, are deeply embedded in the family heritage of many people. As human beings, we have always depended upon the bounty of the earth's natural resources to provide us with the essentials for life: water, sustenance, medicine, building materials, and so on. Foraging helps modern humans to reconnect with our most primal, essential nature—that of being a direct part of nature and natural processes. We are, contrary to what the American culture believes, commensurate with the whole of nature, and by cultivating even the most basic foraging skills, city dwellers, country folk, and everyone in between can benefit from this deeply rewarding and meaningful practice. And for the student of the AODA, one may find that foraging provides an excellent opportunity for enacting the curriculum of the Earth Path of our order. In this article, the reader will learn what foraging is, the basics of foraging, including best-practice procedures, and how foraging can relate to AODA practices. Bear in mind that this is not meant to be an exhaustive guide to foraging; rather it will provide the basic information to build upon and grow in experience.

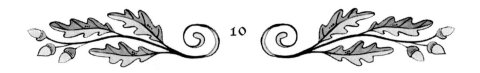

What Is Foraging?

Foraging is an ancient practice, rooted deeply in the collective ancestral and cultural heritage of the human race. In fact, it may very well be the most ancient practice human beings engage in across the whole of the *terra verde*. But what exactly does it mean to forage? Let us first turn to Webster's *Seventh New Collegiate Dictionary* to get a perspective on the roots of the word: "to wander in search of food or forage." This is a good start but seems incomplete.

Foraging, as I personally define it, is as follows: "The act of correctly and safely identifying food and medicine for sustainable harvest in one's environment." One of my earliest memories of foraging was in my youth, around the age of eight or nine, harvesting wild raspberries in the backyard of my parents' semirural Michigan home. Back then, a dense horseshoe-shaped patch of red raspberries grew where the edge of the lawn met the forest. The thorny raspberry canes, as the stems are called, were covered with beautiful red fruits in abundance and packed full of flavor. Despite the fact I didn't catch the bug of becoming an avid forager at that time, it left an indelible mark upon my young mind that has in recent years bloomed into a full-blown, fervent, and passionate love of treading through field and forest, lawn and bog in search of the wonders of nature's bounty.

"Donau Bulgarien und der Balkan" ("Danubian Bulgaria and the Balkan"), Volume I, Leipzig, 1879, p. 238.

The Basics of Foraging

Foraging, much like any discipline or practice, requires a commitment to building the necessary skills, knowledge, and principles in order to become proficient in the art. In essence, the more you learn and apply that knowledge, the more you will grow as a forager. The foundational principles of foraging are relatively simple, and harmonize with AODA practices beautifully. Listed below are five steps to learn foraging:

First, start by reading about edible and medicinal plants growing in your bioregion (your local library may have a nice offering of books to start with). While many great books cover this subject, I think chief among them are the outstanding works of author and expert forager Samuel Thayer: *Nature's Garden* (2006) and *The Forager's Harvest* (2010). I cannot recommend these books highly enough, as they allow the novice to readily and safely identify plants that may be growing in the local ecosystem. His passion for foraging is evident in his books, and his extensive knowledge and detailed photographs and instructions on the art are nothing short of impressive. Buy them, borrow

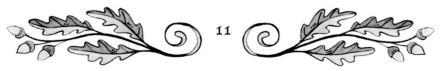

them from a friend, or check them out from your local library—they will provide you with a foundation upon which to build your foraging prowess for years to come. There are no other books like them.

Second, start simple, and, with the help of the aforementioned books (or others like them), learn to properly identify three common edible or medicinal plants that are growing in your locale. Why three plants? First, for practical purposes, learning to properly identify three unique plants is far more manageable than attempting to master a long list. The number three is also magical, and a motif found in many esoteric traditions (e.g., the sulfur, salt, and mercury of Alchemy), and in Druidry, we certainly see this illustrated in the depiction of the three rays of light of the Awen. You will need to learn all of the key characteristics of your three plants—where they grow, what they look like throughout the season, how they taste, how they smell, and when they are to be found and harvested through the seasons. Get to know these plants like the back of your hand so you are 100 percent certain of what you are harvesting, because 1 percent uncertainty can be the difference between edible, poisonous or otherwise. As Thayer says in his books, there are no look-alikes in the plant world, only look-similars. Master those three plants, and their identification, and you will have built a solid foundation that will help you advance yourself as a seasoned forager.

Third, locate a place in your region where these three wild plants grow. It could be in a local city park, a county or state park, or right in your own backyard (bear in mind that one may not be legally allowed to harvest in certain parks). Within due time, and by cultivating a keen and observant eye, the landscape will begin to speak to you, and inform you about where and when to look for the bounty. Here in southeastern Michigan, we have large areas of fields, forests, and wetlands, and there are numerous trees dotting the landscape, including within the cities, all of which afford many opportunities for wild harvesting. In fact, a few common landscaping trees, such as serviceberry, provide a tasty treat hidden in plain sight.

Fourth, visit your selected location and begin the search for the three plants you have studied. Even if you only find one of the three plants, or perhaps none at all, just being outside and tuning into the landscape in search of forage is rewarding in and of itself. Your mind is attuning itself to the environment, and the mental exercise of focusing on a few specific plants is improving your ability to recognize them in the future.

Finally, after you've successfully harvested your first forage, it is a best-practice procedure to eat only a small amount of the plant to see how your body reacts to it. There may be some people whose body may reject one plant, but not another. It is for this reason that you should also try to eat only one type of forage after your first harvest so as to rule out other causes if there is any problem. And from here, you are now empowered with the essentials of foraging, and can begin to explore more deeply what offerings lie in store.

An illustration of Achillea millefolium (Common Yarrow) from *British Entomology* by John Curtis (1828-1840).

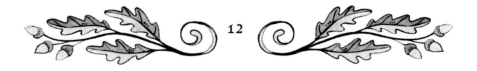

Avoiding Environmental Toxicity

We live a world filled with toxins. This is an established fact, and a trip to your local hardware store, with its containers of deadly toxic "weed" killers will prove this conclusively. When in search of wild foods and medicine, it's of great importance to consider the likelihood of concentrated toxins in the local environment. One of the guiding principles in foraging is always to use common sense, and consider what toxins may or may not be present in your selected foraging area. The local ecosystem in places such as golf courses, around corporate buildings, and so on is known to be regularly doused with poisonous sprays to preserve the austerity of their monocultural lawnscapes, so it's obvious that one should refrain from foraging in these places. Furthermore, railroads and roadsides, among other areas, pose increased risks of environmental toxins, as car exhaust and poor land management strategies pollute the landscapes. The bottom line is, if you have reason to believe you're harvesting in a polluted area, then don't harvest there.

The Ethics of Foraging

Our ecosystems are a delicate balance of give and take, growth and return. Each plant has its own place, established in its own time, and produces a certain amount of growth each season. As such, each plant has its own store of life energy and therefore is capable of giving a certain percentage of itself at each harvest without irreparable harm or injury to itself. With these things in mind, it is of critical importance that we do not take more of a plant than can be easily replenished by the remaining populations in the area, and that we always harvest in a manner that does the least harm to the plant and its surroundings. As a general guideline, it is advisable to harvest only a third of most plants you find, or sometimes less, so as to allow the plant population to regrow and provide future harvests. In the case of fruits, nuts, seeds, and berries, you may harvest with reckless abandon (unless it's a rare plant, which shouldn't be harvested to begin with), for they represent the reproductive bounty of the plants, and pose little risk of overharvest. With this in mind, it's important to leave some behind for other creatures, as the wild harvests are food for our furry friends, and in the case of nuts, it's their winter larder. Foraging is not suited for the "Black Friday" crowd of "Gimme, gimme, gimme, gimme, gimme!" Rather, it is to be a mindful practice in which we endeavor to leave the landscape in the condition in which we found it, if not better, for the same reason we wouldn't allow a guest to squander our food supplies and leave our dwelling space in a state of disarray. Furthermore, it is our sacred duty as Druids to cherish the earth, and treat her well, for she is our gracious, if not presently irritated, host.

Enacting the Earth Path in Field and Forest

How is foraging connected to AODA practice? I feel that foraging is important (and relevant for that matter) for the student of the AODA for at least three reasons:

1. Foraging presents an opportunity for the Druid to enact the Earth Path by developing an active relationship with the natural world. While engaged in the foraging experience, one may take time to enter a state of stillness, silently absorbing all that surrounds one, and then shift into a state of focus, honing in on the patterns on the bark of a tree, or the living geometry of a wildflower in full bloom.

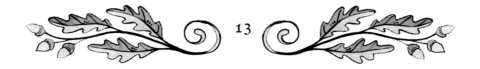

2. It provides motivation and meaningful purpose to be outdoors regularly, which may have therapeutic effects on mind, body, and soul. From the scant records we have of the Druids of the days of old, we can safely say they spent a great deal of time in nature (and they probably knew a thing or two about foraging).

3. The act of foraging can become a form of worship and communion, wherein the Druid is taking part in direct communion with nature, receiving her bounty in a state of reverence and awe.

In my own heart, and in my own mind, I hold foraging to be one of the most enriching, sacred practices I regularly engage in. When wandering through the fields, I behold all around me the glorious beauty of nature, replete with a seemingly infinite diversity of life-forms and complex communities, all living in balance and harmony with nature and nature's law. For me, foraging is not only fun, exciting, and deeply rewarding, it is a vital part of my spiritual practice as a member of the AODA. Though I do learn a lot about foraging from books, or watching videos on the web, I learn and gain more from being engaged in pursuit of the offerings of the land. Being in the wilderness directly informs me about the levels of intelligence in the cosmos, and on our planet, such as when I gaze into a puddle of water, seeing the tiny life-forms dwelling within. Having not pursued higher education after graduating high school, I find myself having enrolled full-time in what I feel to be the greatest of all universities—the natural world. And as such, I have gained so much experience and direct knowledge from these experiences that the act of foraging has taken on deeper spiritual significance that nourishes my soul and enriches my life as a Druid.

Reverence for Nature and the Seasonal Cycles

As Druids, we honor the seasonal changes with celebrations that recognize the shifts taking place on earth and in the heavens. As foragers, we observe these seasonal changes directly as they take place, and the diversity of nature's offerings ebbs and flows. And from the perspective of the foraging Druid, we may arrive at deeper levels of appreciation of the dynamic forces of nature. Below is a summary of each season and what one may expect to glean in each cycle.

Winter

In the wintertime, there are sparse offerings to be found, if any, as it is a time of rest and reflection. This is not to say there aren't edible and medicinal plants to be found; rather, they are supplemental, again supporting the notion that winter is a time of rest. In the Midwestern United States, and elsewhere across the nation where winter entails months of snow, this is all the more applicable. In other parts of the country where there is little to no snow in the winter, one may find that there are many plants to forage for. As I am a native Michigander, I cannot speak to speak that, but I do encourage you to explore what's out there. Plants such as American wintergreen (*Gaultheria procumbens*), with its wonderful flavor and distinct aroma, may be cleared of snow and plucked of leaves (and berries if you're lucky) to use in tasty medicinal teas. In parts of the northern United States, we may find the regal medicinal chaga mushroom (*Inonotus obliquus*) growing high on white birch trees.

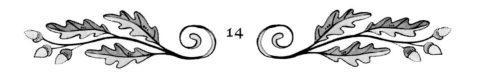

Spring

Come springtime, we begin to see life emerge anew, as tender green plants sprout once more from the newly reawakened earth. The cold, white landscapes of wintertime have given way to a verdant display of life, full of potential. It's an exciting time to harvest, as the air seems fresher, the sun brighter, and the world more vibrant. Not surprisingly, the plants one finds in the spring contain some of the very things our body needs to help us restore ourselves from the prolonged period of winter. There even seems to be a higher life force concentrated in the early growth of spring. Plants such as the beloved dandelion (*Taraxacum officinale*), with its bitter greens, burgeon from the fertile ground, offering us trace minerals and enzymes to help shift our bodies to the changing energies of the season. At this time we also see flower buds open on trees and plants, unveiling a stunningly beautiful world of sacred geometry and brilliant colors. Meanwhile, the Druid forager stands as a witness to this whole process, seeing the seasonal cycles as a sort of cosmic dance or story that gives way to the steamy hot days of summer.

Summer

Summer is when the days are longer, the temperatures hotter, and the diversity of nature's bounty expanded. In my experience, summer presents some of the finest foraging opportunities, as it's the time of year, much like spring, when nature's offerings are best enjoyed at their peak of ripeness. It's the time of year when a variety of wonderful greens and some of the first fruits of the season are ready to enjoy, such as the wondrous wild blueberry (*Vaccinium corymbosum*) with its delicious, antioxidant-rich berries growing on shrubs in knee-deep bogs, to the incredibly flavorful wild strawberry (*Fragaria virginiana*) growing low in fields and lawns; you can't get any fresher than this. And with the sun blazing down on a cloudless afternoon, there's nothing more refreshing than sweet, delicious, and cooling wild fruit. And it's not just fruit that's abundant too, as there are fine wild vegetables to be had, such as the abundant and flavorful wild leek (*Allium tricoccum*), with its onion-like bulb ripe for the picking. Summer also marks the peak of wild gourmet mushrooms, such as the exquisite and flavorful chanterelle (*Cantharellus cibarius*). Mushrooms, however, are not advisable to forage without expert supervision, as they require an advanced level of identification skills. However, numerous mushroom hunting communities nationwide share in this knowledge. As summer begins to cool down, and the long nights draw shorter, the fall beckons onward on this exciting, edible journey.

Autumn

Autumn arrives in a most remarkably beautiful way. The temperatures begin to drop, and the air takes on an earthy aroma, while the trees put on a breathtaking display of incredible colors and hues. It is the time of year when nature is calling us to prepare for the coming winter months by providing us with a wide variety foods that store and preserve well. We again find mushrooms and berries, and we can also find at this time different edible roots and nuts. The shagbark hickory tree (*Carya ovata*), heavy with nuts, drops fruits to the ground, providing us with a flavorful, sustainable source of fats and protein for the coming cold months, while trees like nannyberry (*Viburnum lentago*) bear clusters of delicious, distinctly flavored fruits that can be made into an incredible pudding-like treat that is unlike anything even some of the most adventurous eaters have experienced. And for many of us in

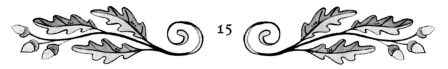

the Midwestern United States, there is the ubiquitous apple tree (*Malus domestica*), with its bountiful, generally sweet fruits that can be preserved in a remarkable number of ways, such as pressing into fresh juice, and fermented to produce an effervescent alcoholic beverage fit for the gods and goddesses. Autumn is also that time of the year when we feast upon the last harvests of the seasons, rejoicing in a year well spent, and to make preparations for the year to come.

Cultivating Stillness and Focus

While engaged in foraging, particularly in the wilderness, the Druid is blessed with the opportunity to be still and to focus. In Earth Path curriculum for candidates, we are to spend fifteen minutes or more in nature each week, taking time to practice stillness and to engage in focus. The Druid forager is afforded rewarding opportunities while in the wilderness to do these practices. For instance, in a city park harvesting acorns beneath an old oak tree, one may take a moment to sit at the base of the tree and become still, taking in the whole experience unfolding around one. This experience may prove to be especially meaningful, as it turns the foraging experience into a spiritual practice. As squirrels hop across the grass, and a passerby walks along the pathways, the Druid sits and takes it all in, without thoughts or words to describe what is unfolding. As a result, a deeper connection to the place is established, and a portion of the necessary meditation is complete.

While still seated in the same place, Druids may shift their awareness and begin to cultivate focus. They may begin to notice the patterns of the blades of grass, the geometry of the acorn caps, the texture of the soil at the base of the tree. Another dimension of experience is attained, and a Druid can completed the requisite meditations while in the middle of adventure seeking food and medicine from the land. Further, the forager develops a set of foraging eyes, a sort of ecological second sight that allows one to read the landscape and identify a plant at a distance, which is quite remarkable and can be attained after a few months of forays into the forests.

Botanical drawing of an alpine strawberry (Fragaria vesca), *The American Cyclopædia*, v. 15, 1879, p. 414.

From Reading Books to Reading the Landscape

During the candidate year, it is necessary that we read nine books on the natural history of the bioregion in which we live, learn about the living things, natural ecosystems, and communities, patterns of weather and water, and development of the

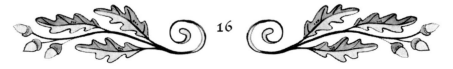

land over time. We are encouraged to relate as much of this information to our own experience of the natural world as possible. We may also see foraging as a useful, practical vehicle for doing just that. We may check out books from our local library, read them at home, or even at a park, and when we embark upon another foraging journey, we may begin to see the very things we read about before us in our pursuit. For instance, after reading a book about local native plants, one may begin to cultivate a relationship with them while walking through a meadow. Suddenly, what was once theoretical knowledge now has become practical, as the flower detailed in the book you just read now appears before you, radiant and full of life. This is where knowledge becomes wisdom, where study becomes direct observation.

The useful information contained in the books we read in our candidate year provides us with tremendous insight and deeper perspectives on our local ecology—a motivation in itself to inspire our journey. Perhaps you live in a town where there used to be acres of orchards, where apples, peaches, and plums once grew in abundance. Maybe one day, you come upon a small park off a dirt road and decide to go explore. As you walk through the wilderness, you suddenly come upon a stand of old apple trees, unpruned, yet still alive as ever. And perhaps you are fortunate enough to arrive when the apple season in is full swing and you come to find the trees you discovered have produced a sizable harvest of excellent quality apples. In a sense, you are biting into a piece of history—a part of the tale that describes what the land once may have been like. And you have the joy of tasting it. In some parts of the United States, including my homeland of southeastern Michigan, this is the case, and I have known the joy of such a scenario.

Making Changes

Another component of the Earth Path is to make three changes in our lifestyles that take less away from the earth and give more back. They should be small yet significant enough that we can maintain them throughout our year as candidates. I am of the opinion that foraging creates the conditions to allow one to enact at least one change in pursuit of nature's yields. By becoming avid foragers, we are helping to reduce our negative impact on the planet by providing at least some of our own food and medicine and, as such, committing to one lifestyle change. We may even extend this notion a step further, and say that we replace watching television with observing nature in our pursuit of wild food and medicine. With no need to turn on the TV, we instead turn to nature to provide us with an experience of far greater significance to our spiritual paths as Druids. Here again, we may find another opportunity for making a lifestyle change. Perhaps you've found a beautiful piece of land, or perhaps a nice little city park within walking distance of your home where a number of edible and medicinal plants await you. This may present an opportunity to make a commitment not to drive a motor vehicle one day a month, or perhaps a week, and this little nook you visit becomes a destination each time you commit to not driving. These are but a few examples of small, creative, and effective changes we can make during our year as candidates.

Extending Our Branches Further

Having undergone the necessary period of study of three plants and observation in the environment, the Druid forager is equipped with the tools necessary to go forth and build upon this foundation of knowledge. Suddenly, or so it seems, new and exciting foraging opportunities emerge, and the natural world appears to be unveiling herself before you—a wonder to behold. Now a walk

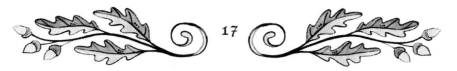

to the store down the roadside becomes an adventure in wildcrafting. A few raspberry canes in a nearby field provide a nice nibble, and the mint growing alongside, with its intense aroma, will make for a fine cup of tea after supper. Upon reaching the destination (the store in this case), a serviceberry (*Amelanchier alnifolia*) tree greets you, hiding right out in the open with its delicious, plump blueberry-esque fruits awaiting you. You take few to snack on before entering the store, and upon leaving, you stop again and fill a small bag to take home with you, perhaps to make a small batch of jam with. While this scenario may not be ecologically possible where you live, the point is this: the Druid forager see nature's gifts wherever plant life is growing and is ready for the occasion to search for her bounty. As such, the world takes on a new perspective—the neighborhood park down the road that may have not held your interest before becomes a place where you pick the wild apples growing. Or perhaps the vacant lot down the block has a nice patch of dandelions that emerge every spring. Whatever the case may be, the Druid now has the skills and confidence to pursue wild offerings in a state of reverence, gleaning from nature what she offers, and leaving the place virtually undisturbed, and perhaps even happy with the company of a mindful human who trod carefully upon her.

Conclusion: Deepening Our Roots in the Earth

As Druids and members of the AODA, we are collectively making small, yet significant changes in our lifestyles, communities, and world that help to reduce our negative impact upon our planet. In a sense, we are striving to deepen our roots in the living earth, not just in our philosophies and spiritual practices, but in our actual corporeal existence as dwellers on this beautiful, mysterious planet we call the earth. In our own ways, we may come to greater and more profound realizations of our interconnectedness with all living things—from the tiniest microbe in the soil, to the depths of the oceans, to the vast mountains towering around us, we are that which we see—nature. It is not possible that it can be any other way. Even the synthetic chemicals manufactured in windowless laboratories, or petroleum products made in hellish factories, are ultimately derived from nature, however perverted and corrupted they may now be. Even the building materials of the very structures where such things take place are of nature. It is humankind that has created a distinction between "man-made" and the natural. However, the two can never be separated. The human race itself is made up of the very elements in the soil, air, and stardust. We are nature. And it is my belief that spending time in nature in the act of foraging helps us to heal our minds, bodies, and souls of the trauma of the declining industrial age. The very act of picking berries from a vine or an herb from the soil allows us to directly interface with that from which all life sprang. As we establish an ongoing relationship with the natural world via foraging, thereby cultivating a relationship to the living land, a process initiates within that helps us regain wholeness in a world where countless humans are disconnected from the source—nature herself.

References

Gove, Phillip (ed) (1967). *Webster's seventh new collegiate dictionary.* Springfield, MA: G.&C. Merriam Co.

Thayer, S. (2006). *The forager's harvest.* Ogema, WI: Forager's Harvest Press.

Thayer, S. (2010). *Nature's garden.* Ogema, WI: Forager's Harvest Press.

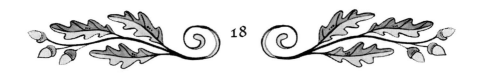

The Myth of Einigan
John Michael Greer

Born in the gritty Navy town of Bremerton, Washington and raised in the south Seattle suburbs, John began writing about as soon as he could hold a pencil. SF editor George Scithers' dictum that all would-be writers have a million words of so of bad prose in them, and have to write it out, pretty much sums up the couple of decades between his first serious attempt to write a book and his first published book, "Paths of Wisdom", which appeared in 1996. These days John lives in Cumberland, Maryland with his spouse Sara; serve as presiding officer -- Grand Archdruid is the official title -- of the Ancient Order of Druids in America (AODA), a Druid order founded in 1912; and writes in half a dozen nonfiction fields, nearly all of them focused on the revival of forgotten ideas, insights, and traditions of practice from the rubbish heap of history.

Every spiritual tradition has its founders; every spiritual tradition also has its black sheep. It so happens that in the case of the Druid Revival, one figure falls into both those categories. Edward Williams (1747–1826), better known during and after his time by his Bardic nom de plume Iolo Morganwg, has the curious distinction of being simultaneously one of the most influential and one of the most despised figures in the history of modern Druidry. His writings remain central to most Druid orders and traditions that date from before the modern Neopagan movement, while most of the Druid orders and traditions that have emerged from contemporary Neopaganism reject Iolo and all his works as mere frauds spun from the raw fibers of eighteenth-century Romanticism.

There's ample justification for a suspicious attitude, at least, toward Iolo's claim to have received Bardic traditions dating back to Celtic antiquity. At the same time, the hardening of attitudes that turned that suspicion into dogmatic rejection may not be justified. As I will show, at least one of the myths that Iolo handed down as an inheritance from antiquity may actually deserve that label, for it contains details Iolo himself could not have identified as relics of the distant past.

The Origins of the Myth

Iolo's lifetime spanned a crucial period in the emergence of the Druid Revival; it was during his time that the first known modern Druid orders appeared and began to attract public notice. Furthermore, he himself contributed greatly to that rise, as the creator of ceremonies and traditions that had an immense impact on the Druid movement then and later.

Until recently, though, these contributions were overshadowed by Iolo's reputation as one of the most glittering stars in the firmament of Romantic literary forgery. There seems to be no doubt that most if not all of the verses and triads Iolo presented as authentic relics of medieval Welsh tradition came from his own busy pen (Constantine, 2007). Some of his creations were not identified as such until the 1950s, and it may well have been a reaction against the resulting embarrassment that led to the blanket condemnation of Iolo by modern scholars.

That condemnation was echoed, and with added heat, in many corners of the modern Druid community. The oversupply of grandmother stories and equally dubious attempts to claim historical legitimacy in the mid-twentieth-century Neopagan scene sparked an inevitable reaction, and Iolo's insistence that his invented Bardic lore dated from time immemorial made him an easy target for

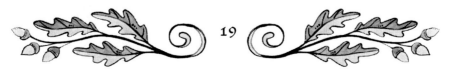

that reaction. It didn't help that some of the Druid orders that used his work most heavily also claimed a direct descent from the ancient Druids they didn't have. Even after the academic community got over its irritation with Iolo and began taking a less one-sided view of his work (see, for example, Jenkins, 2005), many contemporary Druid writers continue to treat Iolo as a fraud pure and simple.

Forgery, though, is a complex thing. Iolo's contemporary and fellow forger James McPherson, to name only one example, wrote a series of long poems, credited them to the legendary figure of Ossian (Oisín in modern Gaelic spelling), and published them as the traditional epic verse of his Highland Scots ancestors. The Ossianic poems were unquestionably McPherson's invention, but the tales of the Fianna on which those poems were based were part of a rich oral and written tradition in Scotland as well as Ireland that is attested long before McPherson's time. Had those tales survived instead only in fragmentary oral form in a few remote corners of the Highlands, the tales as well as the poems might have been dismissed as McPherson's inventions.

The possibility that a similar process might have provided some of the raw material for Iolo's creations has rarely been considered. Still, there is at least one narrative in his published work that is all but impossible to explain if Iolo invented the story out of whole cloth. Nor can that narrative be dismissed as a bricolage of ancient fragments. Rather, it shows the distinctive traces of descent from one of the core mythic patterns of Indo-European antiquity—traces that Iolo, with the resources available in his time, could not have recognized as such.

The Myth in *Barddas*

The narrative in question is the creation myth of Iolo's Bardism, the story of Einigan the Giant and the three rays of light. Originally published in *Barddas*, the posthumous collection of Iolo's papers on Bardic and Druidic teachings, that myth went on to play a central role in many of the later Druid Revival traditions. Here's the clearest of the several versions of the myth included in the published text of *Barddas*:

> *Einigan the Giant beheld three pillars of light, having in them all demonstrable sciences that ever were, or ever will be. And he took three rods of the quicken tree, and placed on them the forms and signs of all sciences, so as to be remembered; and exhibited them. But those who saw them misunderstood, and falsely apprehended them, and taught illusive sciences, regarding the rods as a God, whereas they only bore His Name. When Einigan saw this, he was greatly annoyed, and in the intensity of his grief he broke the three rods, nor were others found that contained accurate sciences. He was so distressed on this account that from the intensity he burst asunder, and with his [parting] breath he prayed God that there should be accurate sciences among men in the flesh, and there should be a correct understanding for the proper discernment thereof. And at the end of a year and a day, after the decease of Einigan, Menw, son of the Three Shouts, beheld three rods growing from the mouth of Einigan, which exhibited the sciences of the Ten Letters, and the mode in which all the sciences of languages and speech were arranged by them, and in language and speech all distinguishable sciences. He then took the rods, and taught from them the sciences—all, except the Name of God, which he made a secret, lest the Name should be falsely discerned; and hence rose the Secret of the Bardism of the Bards of the Isle of Britain. (Williams ab Ithel, 2004, pp. 49–50)*

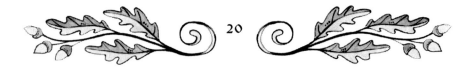

There are several other versions of the same story in *Barddas*. Figuring out their relationship to one another is a serious challenge, because *Barddas* itself is a compilation, assembled after Iolo's death, of various manuscripts of his on the subject of his Bardic mysteries. This raises steep difficulties in the way of any attempt to trace the origins of the stories and lore included in *Barddas*. In most cases, even when there's reason to suspect that a given passage dates from before Iolo's time, there's no easy way to ascertain which of the versions is older, or closer to the putative original. As we'll see, that challenge is commonly faced by students of comparative mythology, and it's precisely by way of comparative mythology that some light can be cast on the myth's origins.

The story of Einigan as given in the various texts, while it's a creation myth, is also a myth concerning the discovery of letters. The three pillars of light—/ | \ in Iolo's as well as later Druid usage—are also the three original letters, spelling out the secret name of God. They are also three vocalizations or voices and three notes of music, as well as the shadow cast by the sun from a post at morning, noon, and evening.

This last meaning had a long afterlife in the Druid Revival, and a great many accounts of nineteenth-century Druidry make astronomical symbolism central to the three pillars of light (see, for example, Morgan, 1890). An oral tradition current in several older Druid Revival organizations equates the head of Einigan and the three rowan staves growing from it with the vault of the heavens and rays cast by three positions of the sun; whether this bit of symbolism dates back to Iolo or not is impossible to answer at this point, as the "Secret of the Bards of the Island of Britain" Iolo referenced so often in *Barddas* and elsewhere, remains secret to this day, part of the inheritance of the Gorsedd y Beirdd—the Welsh Gorsedd of Bards, part of the National Eisteddfod of Wales—and of its daughter gorseddau in Cornwall and Brittany.

The central character of the story, Einigan, is himself something of a mystery. In most of his appearances in *Barddas*, he is the first of all created beings, but one genealogical passage makes him the son of Huon and the great-great-great-grandson of Noah (Williams ab Ithel, 2004, p. 11); a version of the story in Iolo's unpublished papers makes him Menw's son (Constantine, 2007, p. 141), and two versions in *Barddas* make Menw rather than Einigan the witness of the three rays of light (Williams ab Ithel, 2004, pp. 17, 47). I have been able to find no trace of Einigan before Iolo's time, as his other appearances in Welsh literature can all be traced back to Iolo's deft forgeries. Eiddin son of Einigen, for example, is listed as the perpetrator of one of the Three Accursed Deeds of the Island of Britain, but this triad and the whole Third Series to which it belongs are among Iolo's many fabrications.

The name is a puzzle all its own, not least because it appears in several forms in *Barddas*—Einiged, Einiget, Einigan, Einigair, and Einiger. Current French and Breton Druid sources interpret the name as the modern Welsh form of a Gaulish name, Oinogenos, a plausible name (from Proto-Celtic *oino-* "one" and *genos* "born") meaning "firstborn" or "single born."[1] Names of the same structure appear elsewhere in insular Celtic tradition; the name of the Irish god Aenghus, for example, has the same first element—the meaning of the second part of the name is still disputed—and appears in Adomnán's seventh-century *Life of St. Columba* as Oinogusius (Anderson & Anderson, 1991). Whether or not this is the source of the name, though, remains wholly uncertain,

---

[1] Ironically, Oinogenos or Oinogenes is also an attested Greek name, meaning "wine-born," and in ancient times implied having been conceived during a drunken bender (Harris, 2000).

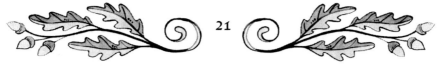

and would not explain the multiple names cited by Iolo.

The Myth in Indo-European Tradition

If we turn from the name to the details of the story, though, we land abruptly in territory familiar to all students of Indo-European mythology. Among the reconstructions of Proto-Indo-European myth, the best known is probably the story of creation. This has two characters, *Mannus (Man)[2] and *Yemos (Twin), who are the first human beings. *Mannus kills and dismembers *Yemos, and makes the world out of the fragments of his body—his bones become the rocks, his skull the sky, his hair the grass, and so on. *Yemos then becomes the king of the dead, while *Mannus becomes the forefather of living human beings (Lincoln, 1975).

This narrative can't be found in intact form in any of the cultures descended from the Proto-Indo-Europeans. What appear instead are fragments of the story, and these can be found both in Indo-European cultures and in the cultures of neighboring peoples: evidence, if any were needed, that a colorful story travels easily. Those of my readers who grew up with the D'Aulaires' colorful *Norse Gods and Giants* will recall the story of the giant Ymir, who was killed and dismembered by the brother gods Odin, Vili, and Ve, and whose parts then became the raw material for the world (Orchard, 2011). Yama in Hindu myth is the first man, who died and became the king of the dead. The *Vendidad*, part of the Zoroastrian sacred scriptures, similarly features a king named Yima Xsaeta, who became the ruler of an underground city that closely resembles the legendary realm of the dead (Darmestetter, 1880).

The *Shah-nameh* of Firdausi, the great epic poem of Persia, includes the story of the great king Jamshid—the name is an exact equivalent of Yima Xsaeta in a later version of the same language—who was sawn in half by the evil Zahhak. The legendary history of Rome, remarkably enough, includes a close copy of the old myth in the tale of the twin brothers Romulus and Remus; Remus's death at Romulus's hands brings about the foundation of Rome rather than the creation of the world, but it's far from uncommon for cosmological myths to be redefined in later eras as foundation legends and the like.

The same myth also found its way into non-Indo-European cultures in the Middle East. (This is far from surprising, as some of the major powers of the ancient Near East, notably the Hittites and the Mitanni, spoke Indo-European languages.) In Babylonia, the hero-god Marduk slays and dismembers the primal being Tiamat and creates the world from the pieces of her body; in the Levant, the Ugaritic texts include an account of Baal's slaying and dismembering of Yam, the ruler of the sea, and it's been argued on a variety of grounds that Psalm 74:13–15 contains an echo of the same mythic narrative, with the Jewish god Elohim slaying and dismembering the sea (in Hebrew as in Ugaritic, Yam). Finally, the Egyptian myth of Osiris, who was killed and dismembered by his brother Set and then became the king of the dead, is arguably another expression of the same mythic pattern. Table 1 sets out these mythological parallels in a convenient form.

The myth of Einigan fits neatly into this family of narratives. It is no more complete than any of the other versions, and like many medieval and modern mythic narratives in the Christian West, it has been reworked to some extent to fit such standard biblical tropes as hostility to idolatry and the

---

[2] In historical linguitsics, an asterisk in front of a word indicates that the word does not appear in any original source and has to be reconstruted by working back from later words descended from it.

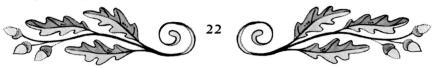

sacred and secret character of the divine name. Its most interesting borrowing from Christian sources, though, appears to derive from the medieval legend of the skull of Adam.

This is found in the *Golden Legend* of Jacobus de Voragine (1230–1298) and a great many other medieval Christian sources. According to de Voragine's version, Seth, son of Adam, visited Paradise and was allowed to take with him three seeds from the Tree of Life. When Adam died, Seth planted the three seeds in his skull, and they sprouted and grew into three trees. The trees were eventually cut down and passed through various vicissitudes before becoming the wood of the cross on which Jesus was crucified. While most of the Christian legend is unrelated to the story of Einigan, the image of three trees growing from the skull of the first man is distinctive enough that some influence, at least, is likely.

This sort of mythological bricolage is a commonplace of comparative mythology, and occurs in several other daughter myths of the story of *Mannus and *Yemos. Einigan's role as the first created being and his dismemberment both reflect the death and destiny of *Yemos, however, as does the identity between his skull and the heavens, if this belongs to the original narrative. The texts in *Barddas* do not identify Menw as Einigan's brother, but the two are coeval; Menw is described as "son of the Three Shouts" (ap Teirwaedd in the original), and the Three Shouts are another form of the three pillars of light, voices, letters, and so on, by which Einigan and the world came into being. Had the story of Einigan and Menw appeared in any less controversial source, it would doubtless have been taken up long ago by comparative mythologists and added to the list of daughter myths the story of *Mannus and *Yemos.

The Origins of an Origin Myth

The obvious question, given Iolo's known proclivities, is whether he could have invented a creation story that echoed the Indo-European pattern well enough to pass for a descendant of original myth. Such things have certainly happened since his time. To name only one instance, the invented mythology of J. R. R. Tolkien includes a typically deft example, in the struggle between the gods Manwe and Melkor that provides the principal plot engine for *The Silmarillion*. Tolkien's professional training as a philologist included close attention to exactly the patterns of Indo-European mythology discussed here, among many others, and it's surely no accident that the victor of the two should have a name closely related to *Mannus, or that the loser should have become the ruler of the underground and distinctly infernal kingdom of Angband, "The Hells of Iron" in Elvish (Tolkien, 1977).

Any such hypothesis about Iolo's possible invention of the Einigan myth, though, runs into a serious difficulty: the reconstruction of Indo-European myth that revealed the parallels just listed had not even begun at the time of Iolo's death in 1826, and was still in its infant stages when *Barddas* finally saw print in 1862. It was in 1786 that Sir William Jones first proposed that Latin, Greek, and Sanskrit, and possibly the ancient Celtic, Germanic, and Iranian languages as well, might all be descended from a common source; the first thorough exploration of the linguistic dimensions of the hypothesis was Franz Bopp's *Comparative Grammar* of 1843; not until the work of linguistic reconstruction was well advanced could comparative mythology get beyond the basics and begin tracing mythic patterns such as the *Mannus-*Yemos myth; and the myth itself was not finally reconstructed from surviving fragments until 1975 (Lincoln, 1975).

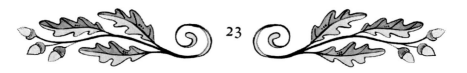

Table 1. Mythological Parallels

Indo-European	*Mannus	killed	his brother	*Yemos	the first man
Roman	Romulus	killed	his brother	Remus	—
Norse	Odin, Vili, and Ve	killed	—	Ymir	the first being
Hindu	Manu	—	—	Yama	the first man
Avestan	—	—	—	Yima Xsaeta	the first king
Iranian	Zahhak	killed	—	Jamshid	—
Babylonian	Marduk	killed	—	Tiamat	the first being
Egyptian	Set	killed	his brother	Osiris	the first king
Ugaritic	Baal	killed	—	Yam	(the sea)
Hebrew	Elohim	killed	—	Yam	(the sea)
Welsh	Menw	—	—	Einigen	the first being

Until that work was done, in turn, faking a creation myth that would fit an Indo-European pattern not yet reconstructed would have been a stunningly difficult challenge. It might be objected that myths of the dismemberment of a primal being were common enough that Iolo could simply have decided to include one, but any such suggestion runs up against a further difficulty: the presence of a name descended from *Mannus in Iolo's myth.

None of the daughter myths that evolved from the Indo-European original, as it happens, put descendants of the names *Mannus and *Yemos in their original positions. The Hindu tradition preserves the name of Manu as the first king and progenitor of humanity, but his role in the death of Yama is nowhere attested; a German myth recorded by the Roman writer Tacitus names Mannus as the forefather of the human race, but lacks the dismemberment motif; a few other mythologies of Indo-European origin echo the name, but their relationship to the Indo-European creation myth was not recognized until long after Iolo's death. Most of the daughter myths, in a pattern long familiar to students of comparative mythology, assign the deed of *Mannus to some more recent or more popular hero or god, while the name of the victim has more commonly survived.

The myth of Einigan, like the other daughter myths referenced above, no longer identifies *Mannus/Menw as the sacrificer and dismemberer of *Yemos/Einigan. The two are still clearly connected by the narrative, however, as they are in very few other sources—and in no source available to Iolo during his lifetime. Here again, had the narrative of Einigan and Menw appeared first in a less controversial source, this detail would have guaranteed it a significant spot among the surviving traces of the original Indo-European myth.

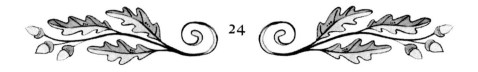

who was dismembered	became king of the dead	and from his body the cosmos was made
—	—	Rome was founded
who was dismembered	—	and from his body the cosmos was made
—	became king of the dead	—
—	became king underground	—
who was sawn apart	—	—
who was dismembered		and from her body the cosmos was made
who was dismembered	became king of the dead	—
who was dismembered	—	—
who was dismembered	—	—
who burst asunder	—	(and his head became the heavens)

Though Iolo Morganwg's gifts as a poet, a scholar of medieval Welsh, and a forger were by no means minor, his surviving work does not support the claim that he was among the most gifted comparative mythologists in history. Yet something like this would have been required to allow him to successfully reconstruct an archaic Indo-European myth, create a plausible Welsh descendant of that myth, and muddle it together with scraps of medieval legend in a highly convincing manner, a century and a half before anyone else could have done so. The most likely hypothesis instead is that he stumbled across some fragment of genuinely ancient lore in his studies of medieval and early modern Welsh poetry and culture, and added it to the mass of inventions and borrowings that became his system of Bardic lore.

The casual dismissal of Iolo as a simple forger and fraud thus clearly requires some degree of revision. That conclusion by no means justifies a swing to the opposite extreme, since much of what appears in Iolo's oeuvre was unquestionably his own creation. Rather, the points I've tried to raise here suggest that a much more nuanced understanding of Iolo's achievement is needed—an approach that considers the ingredients of his Bardic system individually, on their own terms, and uses the full range of scholarly tools to sort out possible scraps of older lore from Iolo's inventions and interpretations.

Within the modern Druid community, by contrast, a more straightforward approach may be helpful. The spiritual and personal validity of a myth does not depend on its historical origins; rather, it depends on the myth's resonance with personal and collective experience, and with the teachings and values of traditions that consider the myth a sacred narrative. Taken on its own terms, as a teaching story, as a theme for meditation, or in any of the other ways myths are used in living spiritual traditions, the myth of Einigan has plenty to offer. The possibility that it might reflect mythic patterns dating back to Indo-European antiquity has no effect on its value in these terms—though it does bring a certain additional interest to the tale.

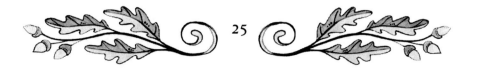

References

Adams, D. Q., & Mallory, J. P. (1997). *Encyclopedia of Indo-European culture*. London: Taylor and Francis.

Anderson, A. O., & Anderson, M. O. (Ed. & Trans.). (1991). *Adomnán's life of St. Columba*. Oxford: Oxford University Press.

Constantine, M.-A. (2007). *The truth against the world: Iolo Morganwg and romantic forgery*. Cardiff: University of Wales Press.

Darmesteter, J. (Trans.). (1880). *The Vendidad*. In M. Muller (Ed.), *The sacred books of the east*, Vol. 4, *The Zend-Avesta, Part 1*. Oxford: Oxford University Press.

Harris, W. V. (2000). A Julio-Claudian business family? *Zeitschrift für Papyrologie und Epigraphik, 130*, 263–264.

Jenkins, G. H. (Ed.). (2005). *A rattleskull genius: The many faces of Iolo Morganwg*. Cardiff: University of Wales Press.

Lincoln, B. (1975). The Indo-European creation myth. *History of Religions, 15*(2), 121–145.

Morgan, O. (1890). *The light of Britannia*. Cardiff: Daniel Owen.

Orchard, A. (Trans.) (2011). *The Elder Edda: A book of viking lore*. New York: Penguin Classics.

Tolkien, J. R. R. (1977). *The Silmarillion*. New York: Ballantine.

Williams ab Ithel, J. (Ed.). (2004). *The Barddas of Iolo Morganwg*. Boston: Weiser.

A Local Ogham: Finding Your Area's Sacred Plants
Dana Wiyninger

Dana Wiyninger received a BS in Conservation of Natural Resources from the University of California, Berkeley in 1979. Following a career in local environmental regulation, she and her husband are restoring their forested land and traveling throughout North America. She is a member of the Order of Bards, Ovates and Druids (Druid grade), the Reformed Druids of Gaia, and the AODA (Druid apprentice). For the last decade her blog, Danaan: Sacred Nature, has explored nature and spiritual practice. She has also been a volunteer administrator of the unofficial AODA Facebook page since 2009.

My Druid studies include the Ogham (or Ogam), an ancient Irish alphabet using sacred trees. Today, the Ogham has traditional and new symbolic associations; and while often used for divination, it is a wonderful tool for finding the sacred in the plants where you live. Note that the Ogham includes what we would call both plants and trees—I use the traditional "trees" here.

The teachers in one of my Druid orders advised that I go out and physically find the Ogham trees, and with direct observation and communion learn their lessons directly before any study of established spiritual associations. This is fine direction when you live in the traditional area for these trees—Ireland, the United Kingdom, and thereabouts. Given the vast variation of plants across the world, seeking the Ogham trees is difficult for most of us. For example, the UK has four ecoregions, while Australia has forty, and the United States has over 104.

I found myself in this quandary; not only did I not live in Europe, but I moved from California to Florida, states with widely varying ecosystems. The seventeen acres of forested Florida land my husband and I moved to had been unmanaged for nearly fifty years; we decided to restore it to a more healthy and natural state for wildlife and related uses. That process required consultations with foresters, study, formal training, and regular fieldwork. Luckily, learning about local plants and forest health was a good preparation for finding my own Ogham trees. Starting out, I did not know how far I would eventually go with my Ogham studies. As they progressed, I received inner urging from my guides to develop a local Ogham that could be shared. Even with all of the hard work, I found the study of the Ogham to be very worthwhile, and highly recommend finding your own trees in your ecoregion.

Since I came up with my Florida Ogham[3] people have asked me about Oghams for their areas. While I know of a few local versions, not many are available (see my list at the end of the article). I have also been to a Druid gathering where we were discussing the yew in the Ogham (Ioho), and people said, "There are no yew trees here." When I asked what local equivalent tree they did have, I got blank stares. I would like to help change that.

So, in an effort to help others find an Ogham for their areas, here is the process I used to develop mine. I found I needed many steps just to find my local trees before I could start my formal Ogham studies. There are twenty-five or more Ogham trees, and I studied two to three times that many local trees; so working on a local Ogham can be quite involved. You may find other ways that

---

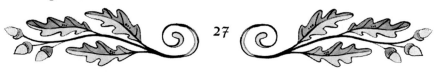

work for you, or decide to break up your study into small Ogham letter (few) groups (aicme), but this should give ideas on how to proceed in developing your own area Ogham.

Define Your Geographical Area

Use elevation, plant communities, distance, climate zones (USDA zones in the United States), ecoregions, and the like to choose your area. Remember that the ancients did not have all of the Ogham trees in their literal backyard. Many of the Ogham trees are significant for the physical place they occupy (for instance, willow/Saille at the boundary of earth and water), and we need to travel to find them. This process may help you know your geographic area better, and you may find yourself changing how you define it for your Ogham.

For example, my part of Florida has only one ecoregion, and forested areas have been relatively undisturbed, so I was able to find plenty of trees to study in my local area. Conversely, where I used to live in California was at the boundary of three ecoregions, in a landscape that had been drastically disturbed by historic gold mining, and with plant communities that differed with elevation. If I had continued my Ogham studies there I likely would have included a larger area along a swatch of northern California to the coast (in part to include the coast redwoods).

Image 1: American Holly, Tinne (*Ilex opaca*). Photo courtesy of USDA NRCS.

Choose What Type of Plants to Include

Decide if you are going to start off including existing natives only, or existing and historical natives, or natives and introduced (exotic) plants. The geographical area you have chosen may have a multitude of native trees suitable for your Ogham. Or your wildlands may have few suitable native trees, but have many nonnative (or exotic) ones. Exotic plants are sometimes purposefully introduced, and may now safely fill the niche of an extinct or depleted native tree. However, other exotics are unintended or invasive plants that cause widespread plant species depletion and damage to the local ecosystem. (It's easy to learn about invasive plants in your area—the local agricultural extension service will have a list and information on them.)

You may find historical native trees that are extinct or rare, and you may want to acknowledge them in your Ogham. The Ogham is an integrated system, so finding trees that are in balance with your forest would be best, in my opinion. I had plenty of native trees to study in Florida, and chose

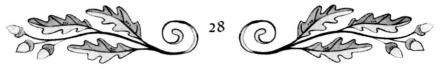

not to include some plentiful and beautiful invasive exotic plants in my Ogham. With fewer types of related native trees in my area of northern California, I would have expanded my geographical region to find more prospects. Just realize that after you have gone through the process of finding specific trees, you might end up revising the types of trees to include.

Study the Traditional Ogham Trees

In preparation for finding your area Ogham, I found it useful to learn the plant family and growth characteristics of the traditional Ogham trees. This means learning about the fun world of scientific plant and plant family names in Latin, but there is a good reason to do this. Common names can be shared among many trees, so they can't be used when you are trying to be specific. There can be huge variation across a single group, like oaks (family beech or Fagaceae, genus *Quercus*), which has about 900 species worldwide. You need to start by knowing what oaks the traditional Ogham uses before you go looking for a local tree. The botanical names of the traditional UK Ogham trees are available in my Florida Ogam (which are the ones used by the Order of Bards, Ovates and Druids, based in the UK), and John Michael Greer's *The Druidry Handbook*, among other sources.

Using the scientific names, UK tree guides, and online sources can help you gain a general understanding of the traditional Ogham trees themselves. Basic tree characteristics include:

- Seasonal life cycles of the trees (when they leaf out, when they fruit, how long they keep leaves, etc.)
- Being evergreen (looking alive in the winter)
- Color of bark, fruits, flowers, and sap (white and red are often significant in Celtic lore)
- The place they occupy in the landscape (in wet or dry conditions, single or in groves, height, etc.)
- Growth habit
- General nature and use of the wood or other parts (Note: finding direct equivalence between UK and other trees based on medicinal uses is difficult—and certainly only a small part of the aspects that make up an Ogham tree.)

For example, the traditional Ogham oak is often noted as being the *Quercus rober* or *Quercus petraea* trees—both large, spreading, long-lived, deciduous (losing leaves in winter), acorn-bearing oaks supporting a high diversity of other life forms. They are usually the dominant tree in their area (unlike many oaks elsewhere).

Use Local Plant Guides to Find Similar Local Trees

I found local plant guides that were organized by plant family to be very useful, as plants in the same family or genus will share many growth, form, flowering, habitat, and other features. Looking up local trees before going out into the field will help; it will let you know if you have several candidates from the same plant family as the Ogham tree you are looking for, or if you will have to look harder for an unrelated plant that you find has similar characteristics.

Using the example of oaks, you might find many oaks in your area but only one or two that are large, long-lived, deciduous, and home to lots of other plants and animals. If you don't have local oaks you can look up other trees in the same family, or look for trees that share characteristics with

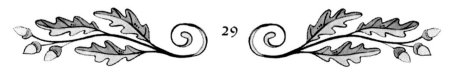

the traditional trees. Researching your local plant guides will help you know where to start and how many local trees you want to investigate for each Ogham tree. Note that it is useful to run your alternate trees through the following steps in this article—you may find them useful to fill a gap in your Ogham later.

Survey Local Trees in the Field

This is where it gets fun! You take your guides and lists of candidate trees and go into your neighborhood, parks, nature areas, and botanical gardens (a great resource if you have one) and locate your trees. Some may be easy to find, along with many related candidates. Other trees might be absent, and you may have to find new alternatives in related genera, or in other plant families. I found taking notes and photos to be useful. I also started putting some of the information into spreadsheets after it came to me that I would be sharing what I found—keep the type of records that work for you.

During my survey I had to cross off some candidate trees that are endangered and not found in the wild anymore, or that are too dissimilar to the traditional Ogham tree. When this happened I went out to survey alternate trees, some of which later became my main candidate trees.

Observe and Get to Know Your Ogham Trees

This is where living in an area for some time would be helpful. If you are born and raised in your area you may already know when trees leaf out, what fruits they have, how they sound in the wind, and the like. Observe all of these things for your candidate and alternate trees, and how they "feel" to you.

This is when the nexus between the science of finding an Ogham tree candidate and the art of finding the tree's spirit will kick in. Spend time with your tree; meditate with it; remember any associations you have for it. For example, what tree did you sit under as a child? How did it make you feel? In this culture and as adults we tend to lose this connection with our plants—you are now building these connections.

You may also find that trees will give differing impressions based on the area they are in, or their age. For example, one of my Florida trees, black cherry (*Prunus serotina*), which started out as an alternative tree, came through more clearly after I found a large mature specimen to start visiting with. There are various ways to connect, but opening yourself and being with the trees is the way to start. Give this phase the time it needs. (When my UK teachers said to know the Ogham trees first—to directly observe and commune with them—it is this step. With finding local trees, this ends up as my sixth step.)

Develop Ogham Associations for Your Candidate Trees

Knowing your trees to some degree now, do you get any impressions from them? Try asking them if they have any messages for you. Write down any feelings, impressions, poems, or the like that come to you. Keep on visiting your trees. Even though I have steps after this one, it is this connection and relationship with your trees that is central to any Ogham. You may find that this stage will help you decide which tree to choose from several candidates, or make you broaden your search.

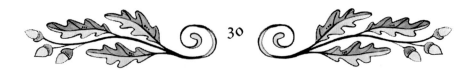

I had two oak candidates in Florida by this step. It was the larger, more long-lived oak (laurel oak, *Quercus hemisphaerica*) that resonated most strongly with me, having an aura of strength and protection. These impressions only strengthened for me over time.

Compare Traditional Ogham Associations to Your Tree Associations

Now that you have found your local candidate trees, you can start to study the traditional and modern Ogham symbolism and associations. While each Ogham few (letter) is tied to a tree, many other ancient and modern associations have also been applied. You will also find variations across authors or individuals, which is fine. When you compare other associations you will likely find they differ from yours. What others have done may clarify your impressions, or yours may just arrive at a different tangent than theirs. I found my tree associations to be pretty close to those found by others, but it will vary by Ogham few. (Studying the traditional Ogham was the second step my UK teachers said to do after I personally knew the Ogham trees. With finding local trees, this ends up as my eighth step.)

I also found studying UK Ogham tree lore helpful in explaining or expanding on published Ogham associations. Additional associations (like colors, birds, and animals) have been used with the Ogham, making it a rich tool for divination or other practice. Given our many varied ecosystems and lands, you may well find valid new associations of your own to add to your Ogham.

Review and Finalize Your Ogham

Using the traditional associations as a check, you may find you need to reevaluate and find another local tree that more closely matches the traditional interpretation and growth characteristics for that Ogham tree. When this happened, I used alternate trees from my list, other trees that I put through the process (for fun), or did more research and put new trees through the above steps.

You can take time to just go over your notes, check in with the trees themselves, and adjust to see how everything fits. This can include revising your geographic area; revisiting your native and/or exotic trees decision; finding new research resources; new field reviews; more observation of your trees through the seasons; and additional study of the traditional Ogham associations. (This sounds hard, but I do not think you will find it so by the time you're at this stage.) Realize that as your area knowledge and connection grows you can revisit your Ogham and refine it in the future.

By the time I developed my list, I was surprised that I was able to find similar plants for about half of the UK Ogham trees in Florida. But that means that the other half of my Ogham are from other plant families. In those cases, I was able to find native trees that had a similar form, growth habit, and impression as the traditional Ogham trees. I did run one exotic plant through the process—the camphor tree (*Cinnamomum camphora*)—but found it didn't align with any Ogham tree (or even with a definable niche, which is probably why it is an invasive plant in north and central Florida). Of course, there are plenty of other plants that are worthy of study apart from use in an Ogham system. In the last year I have added more lore to some of my Ogham fews, and perceive that my Ogham studies will certainly continue.

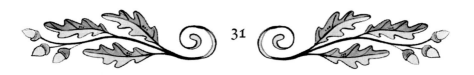

Local Versions of Ogham

If you decide to go through all of this work, you may discover that this is just an entry into the many marvels and lessons of nature. I found that the study of the Ogham yields rare rewards. There are some available local versions of the Ogham; I have listed a few here to inspire others to develop their own:

> A Pacific Northwest Ogham. (2003). John Michael Greer.
> > http://aoda.org/Articles/A_Pacific_Northwest_Ogham.html
> Dryadia's Native Texas Oghams. (2007). Dryadia.
> > http://dryadia.webs.com/
> An Australian Ogham. (n.d). Taran.
> > http://www.druidry.org/library/trees/australian-ogham
> Ogam and Native Florida Plants. (n.d). Dana Wiyninger.
> > http://danaan.net/ogam-fl/

Resources

Here are some online and print resources to use in developing a local Ogham. Many of these are specific to North America, but they may point the way to resources for other regions.

Plants

> Plants and Fungi. Kew Royal Botanic Gardens. Retrieved from
> > http://www.kew.org/science-conservation/plants-fungi
> Explore Plants. Native Plant Information Network. University of Texas at Austin. Native
> > wildflowers, plants and landscapes throughout North America. Retrieved from
> > http://www.wildflower.org/explore/
> PLANTS Database. US Department of Agriculture. Standardized information about the
> > vascular plants, mosses, liverworts, hornworts, and lichens of the United States and
> > its territories. Retrieved from http://plants.usda.gov/java/
> Fire Effects Information. USDA Forest Service. (Also look up your local agricultural
> > extension and state or territory forestry programs.) Retrieved from
> > http://www.fs.fed.us/database/feis/plants/
> North American Native Plant Society. Local chapters will have members who can help
> > with plant identification during meetings and field trips. Retrieved from
> > http://www.nanps.org/index.php/resources/native-plant-societies
> US Land Cover Vegetation Map. US Geological Survey and University of Idaho. Retrieved
> > from http://www.gap.uidaho.edu/landcoverviewer.html
> U.S. National Vegetation Classification. US Geological Survey. Retrieved from
> > http://usnvc.org/explore-classification/
> List of Botanical Gardens and Arboretums in the United States. Wikipedia. Retrieved
> > fromhttp://en.wikipedia.org/wiki/List_of_botanical_gardens_and_arboretums_in
> > _the_United_States

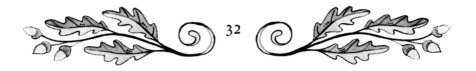

List of Canadian Plants by Family. Wikipedia. You can also search at Wikipedia by plant family. Retrieved from http://en.wikipedia.org/wiki/List_of_Canadian_plants_by_family

Category: Lists of Ecoregions by Country. Wikipedia. Retrieved from http://en.wikipedia.org/wiki/Category:Lists_of_ecoregions_by_country

Uses

Native American Ethnobotany. A Database of Foods, Drugs, Dyes and Fibers of Native American Peoples, Derived From Plants. University of Michigan–Dearborn. Retrieved from http://herb.umd.umich.edu/

Ogham and Tree Lore

Trees. Order of Bards, Ovates and Druids. Some individual tree lore and ogham information. Retrieved from http://www.druidry.org/library/trees

Greer, J. (2006). *The Druidry Handbook*. San Francisco: Red Wheel/Weiser.

Ogham (2014) in Wikipedia. Retrieved from https://en.wikipedia.org/wiki/Ogham

Paterson, J. (1996). *Tree Wisdom: The Definitive Guidebook*. London: Thorsons.

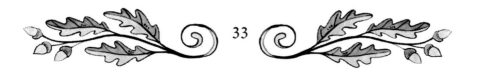

Learning and Using the Sphere of Protection: Daily Practice, Energetics, and Advanced Workings

Dana Lynn Driscoll

Dana Lynn Driscoll is the Chief Editor of Trilithon: The Journal of the Ancient Order of America *and a Druid Adept in the AODA. She also is Druid grade graduate in the Order of Bards, Ovates, and Druids, a member of the Druidical Order of Golden Dawn, and a Deacon in the Gnostic Celtic Church. Her AODA Druid Adept project explored the connection between druidry and sustainability and how to use permaculture design principles and community building to engage in druidic practice. By day, she is a writing professor and learning researcher; by night, an organic gardener, natural builder, mushroom forager, herbalist, and whimsical artist. Dana's writings can be found on the web at druidgarden.wordpress.com.*

The Sphere of Protection (SOP) is the primary magical working in the AODA and is to be learned and practiced daily. Extended work on any magical practice is a deeply personal experience—how the SOP will work for you will be unique to you and you alone. In this article, I share my experiences and advanced workings of the SOP based on years of practice with the goal of providing new insights into this ritual at the core of AODA practice.

The Sphere of Protection Ritual

The SOP functions as a basic magical protection, energizing, and balancing ritual. It is also used in both the AODA's solitary grove opening and standard grove opening rituals. Basic instruction in the SOP can be found in several places—the AODA's website provides a basic overview of the SOP (Gilbert & Greer, 2003), while an advanced version is found in the *Druid Magic Handbook* (Greer, 2007). If you want to take the SOP as a serious daily practice—and possibly use it in other ways, as I describe below—I strongly recommend using the *Druid Magic Handbook* to learn and explore the SOP.

For readers new to the SOP, I provide a brief description of it here; however, this short description is not meant as instructions for learning the SOP (for that, see the references). The SOP has three main parts: the Elemental Cross, the invocation of the gates, and the Circulation of Light. The SOP also includes three kinds of actions: visualization and energetic work, verbal phrases, and physical movement. First, the Druid begins by invoking the elements or deity and physically and energetically forming an Elemental Cross. Second, the Druid invokes the four elemental gateways by invoking positive qualities of the four elemental energies (Air, Fire, Water, Earth) and banishing the negative qualities of those elements. The Druid then invokes the remaining three gateways: the telluric current (Spirit Below), the solar current (Spirit Above), and the lunar current (Spirit Within) using language, action, and visualization. The final part of the SOP draws upon these seven energies and circulates light in a protective sphere. This protective sphere is most typically placed around a person or a sacred grove in order to do ritual work, but it can have many other uses, some of which are explored in this article.

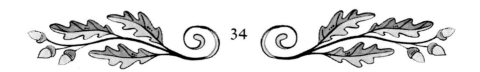

Sphere of Protection Painting (acrylic on fabric) by Dana Driscoll

The Importance of Learning and Doing the SOP as a Daily Practice

Doing the SOP each day helps you establish a daily spiritual practice. Over the years, I have experimented with many ways of integrating the SOP and other daily practices into my life. I tried it as the last thing before bed, the first thing in the morning, on my lunch hour at work, before taking a bath, and so on. This experimentation led me to understand that the SOP is a very flexible, powerful ritual that can effectively be done at numerous points in the day and used in numerous ways. In the end, I decided to use the SOP as my morning practice. The first thing I do when I wake up is walk the five or so feet from my bed to my altar, light candles and incense, and begin my day with a short meditation, the SOP, and a daily divination. By the time I'm done with the meditation, I'm fairly alert, and when I finish with the SOP, I am ready to tackle the day. I have found that doing the SOP in the morning sets a positive, balanced tone for each day; it sends me into the world with protection and energizes me. I usually set aside twenty minutes for this morning work, and I find that the short dedication of daily time has far-ranging benefits.

The same kinds of dedication and practice needed to learn an instrument and play it with effect apply to learning any magical practice, including the SOP. You are also going to see improvements with practice—and only with practice. The more you perform the same ritual, the stronger the ritual becomes and the more intimate part of your spiritual practice the working becomes. Furthermore, the more you perform the same ritual in the same physical location, the easier it becomes to perform that ritual because you are establishing energetic connections (called tracks in space in some esoteric circles).

The effects of a magical daily practice, like the SOP, occur at many levels, not all of them obvious. When I first came to Druidry, I had literally no background in any of the Western esoteric traditions, and I wasn't sure what to expect. I began practicing the ritual during my candidate year (not always daily, which was the first problem) and, at first, I didn't feel it was very effective. Looking back, part of the reason I wasn't feeling its effects was that I was still

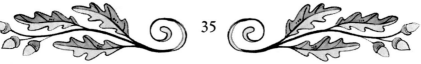

building my energetic senses, and I wasn't fully aware of what was occurring within and around me as I worked the SOP. But the other part was that the SOP started by working at an internal, energetic level—each day, it quietly worked to help bring in the right combination of balanced elemental energies, a process that takes time. It wasn't until I had achieved a certain inner balance that I began to sense that balance and later to sense my SOP at work in the broader world. I see this early work now almost like a glass of water, being filled one drop at a time. A few days of practice may not be noticeable, but a few weeks of practice will reveal water in the bottom of a cup, and a few months or years later, you'll have more than enough to drink.

Over the years, my own SOP has evolved many times. The more serious I grew about practicing it, the stronger it became. The more I dedicated myself to taking the time each day to perform it, the more I noticed its effects. Furthermore, as I performed it, the more it evolved into my own unique version—the visualizations grew more complex, the energies that I was able to banish and summon grew in magnitude, and the protections I was able to create grew in strength and magnitude.

This is all to say that the most important thing you can possibly do is dedicate yourself to daily practice of the SOP. Even if you don't think you are seeing results, keep doing the work. It may take time for the ritual to manifest direct results in your life that you can sense, but it doesn't mean that the ritual isn't working.

The SOP and Energetic Blockages

You may find the SOP challenging to perform early on, or you might not see the kinds of effects that you are expecting, for several reasons. This section covers two major energetic challenges—external and internal energetic blockages—that I faced early on and how I overcame them.

Internal blockages can prevent us from reaching our full magical and spiritual potential, which was certainly something I had to overcome. When I started the path of Druidry, I was coming out of agnosticism, which was my reaction to growing up in a fundamentalist and evangelical home. Even though I had had a set of experiences that made me unquestionably understand that there was a spiritual dimension deeply rooted in nature beyond the material realm, I was still having trouble believing in the work when I started my Druidic path. As long as I continued to ask if "this stuff is even real," I was blocking much of the progress I could make with the SOP. In time and with many deep experiences, I was able to overcome that particular hurdle and move forward with my SOP and other Druidic work.

External blockages are a second serious challenge to effective daily magical practice. For a good portion of my seven-year path as a Druid, I was in a long-term relationship with an atheist who, unfortunately, grew increasingly unsupportive. I had difficulty doing any magical work when he was around, and I also discovered that the SOP could not be done as effectively in the house where we lived. When I went outside into the sacred stone circle I had built far from the house, the SOP was much more effective. Since the SOP works on an energetic level, when you or or someone in your life is blocking those energies, it becomes much harder to gain all of the positive effects. It's like trying to paddle a kayak upstream—if you are paddling upstream, you'll make very limited progress, but your muscles will grow much stronger in the process. The SOP still had its effects during this period of my life—in this case, it helped to shield me from some of the worst of the negative effects of our challenged relationship. When the relationship ended and those energetic blocks were severed, it was like the SOP exploded out of me in brilliant flashes of light. All those years doing the

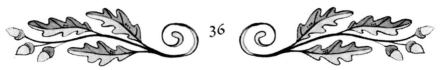

SOP in difficult energetic circumstances had, to use the kayak metaphor, made my muscles quite strong. And when the resistance factor was gone, my SOP became incredibly effective in a very short amount of time—and it continues to grow with each passing day.

Evolving Visualization and Energetic Work

One of the benefits of doing the work of the SOP on a daily basis is seeing its evolution over time. When I started doing the SOP, it was very "by the book" in the sense that I used the suggested visuals and language on the AODA website and, later when it was published, in the *Druid Magic Handbook*. As I built my own connections with the elements, animals, and deity, I slowly adapted the SOP to my specific path (a process furthered by the *Druid Magic Handbook*).

I've found that the evolution of my SOP sometimes happened without my conscious influence. For example, in calling each of the four elements, I worked up to visualizing the symbol and a simple scene in that quarter (in the yellow gate of Air, this was a nondescript hawk soaring in puffy white clouds with the breeze blowing). When I moved to a new state after several years of practicing the SOP, the hawk, of his own volition, took on qualities of the sharp-shinned hawk, a dominant hawk in my new region. I saw him first in my SOP, then out in the wild by the side of the road, and it took me some time to identify what he was. Over time, I began also seeing visual effects in the SOP that I hadn't consciously created—leaves blowing at my feet in the fall months, grasses growing and bending in the breeze, rain falling when I called the powers of Water, and so forth.

Another example of the evolution of the SOP is the result of using the Circulation of Light to protect my home and property. The protective sphere, which I reinforce each day, took on numerous qualities that I hadn't envisioned there—it grew thorny vines and those vines, over a period of months, budded and flowered. Then a great number of bees showed up to pollinate the flowers of the sphere, and so on.

The Many Uses of the SOP

The SOP is truly a complete ritual in its own right and, as such, it can be used in many ways. I would suggest to readers that beyond self-protective work, much of what I discuss in this last part of the article constitutes advanced practices that should be done only after you are comfortable with the SOP and have been practicing it for some time.

The SOP as a Magical Protective Practice

Three of the main uses of the daily SOP is to summon and balance elemental energies, connect with the three currents in the land, and provide a protective shield. I have found that as my Druidic path deepened and as I grew more spiritually connected and sensitive, the need for a daily protective practice increased. I was always sensitive to my surroundings, and Druidry made me even more so (there are many great benefits to this increased sensitivity, but it also has its drawbacks). Regardless of whether I leave home or stay in, I want to make sure that I always have that magical protective buffer. This is particularly important in the fast-paced, materialistic, postindustrial world we find ourselves in, where individual actions and broader cultural movements are actively harming the lands we hold sacred, and when a rather negative cultural and political climate dominates. I recall a time recently when I decided I was too sick to do my daily SOP in the morning and opted to stay in bed. Later in the day, I decided to drag myself out to the doctor. The difference I felt in interacting in the

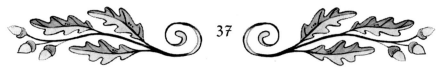

world without that reinforced sphere that day was striking—not just the illness, but the feeling of spiritual drain that normally I did not experience.

In addition to a daily practice, you can also use the SOP when you are feeling unbalanced or in need of more protection throughout your day. The SOP will help you get rid of excess or unwanted energy or bring more positive energies into your life. That's the beautiful nature of the SOP ritual; because it invokes, banishes, and protects, it has many different benefits and can be drawn upon for a variety of protective circumstances.

Using the SOP to Balance, Protect, and Heal People and Places

In addition to using the SOP as a personal protective and balancing ritual, once you are able to perform the SOP with effect, you can use it to balance and protect other people and spaces as needed (on a limited basis). I've used it primarily to protect, heal, and balance spaces—when I do my daily SOP, I also expand the sphere to include my land and property, as I mentioned earlier. I've also used it to help balance a sick friend's energies—and it is effective for this purpose.

I want to describe an experience of the powerful effects of the SOP in working with desecrated lands. Recently, a fellow Druid friend and I went on a magical journey at Samhuinn. One of the places that we visited was White Rock, a large rock located in southeastern Michigan on the western shore of Lake Huron. White Rock is very sacred to several Native American tribes (including the Ojibawa), who used to hold councils, ceremonies, and offer sacrifices to the spirits on the rock. While White Rock has an unfortunate history of disrespect on the part of non-Natives spanning all the way back to colonial times, the U.S. military engaged in the worst kind of desecration by using the rock as a bomb target practice site for their World War II air strikes.

My friend and I had been feeling led to visit White Rock for over a year, and we both knew that we were being sent there to do some land healing and energetic work, but the nature of the healing work wasn't revealed to us in advance. When we arrived, I suggested we start with the SOP to help balance the energies and clear the space for further work, and she firmly agreed. As I started performing the SOP, it became quite clear to us both that the SOP was the main magical working we were meant to do there, and the two of us spent quite a bit of time invoking and banishing the energies of that space and establishing the protective sphere. The energies of Fire were particularly unbalanced (likely because of all of the bombings) and with the help of our guides, spirits of the land, and deity, we were able to bring them back into balance. What we had thought was a way to open the space for further magical work ended up being the work itself. This is not to say that our work at White Rock is finished—we know it isn't. But we do know that the SOP was the start of that healing process. In fact, it was this particular event that led me to write this article.

The SOP can be used to protect a larger space, temporarily or more permanently. I have found that the size of the area is only one factor in what can be protected, and energetics are another. The area might require balancing and energetic work for some time before the protective sphere can be firmly established—for larger spaces, I protect them at regular intervals and seek aid of the spirits of place and the powers of the elements for furthering this work.

The SOP can also be effective for distance healing. I've experimented with this myself and have seen its positive results firsthand with members of my family. Numerous discussions on the AODA listserv have resulted in John Michael Greer suggesting, "The Sphere of Protection makes a very good distance healing ceremony. Simply invoke healing energy and banish illness and harm during

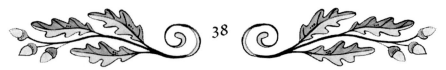

the working of the seven gates, and then when you've finished, imagine the sphere contracting into a ball and project it toward the person who needs help, visualizing it flying through space to that person and expanding to surround them" (Greer, 2009).

The SOP for Magical Crafting and Bardic Arts

Another way that I use the SOP is to establish spaces for magical crafting and the practice of bardic arts. When I have the intent of making a magical object (a tooled leather bag, a set of runes, a magical painting, a tincture, a pendant, etc.), I use the SOP to help me balance the energetics of the space and pull in what is needed for the project (the focus of Air, the steady hands of Earth, the spark of inspiration of Fire, the vision and connection of Water). Depending on what I am making, I might craft in an open AODA solitary grove (which, of course, uses the SOP) or I might just do the SOP on its own. My choice in this depends partially under what circumstances I am crafting—if a non-Druid friend is joining me, I might just use the SOP before the friend arrives to create a nice crafting space, but if I am alone or with a friend who would support such work, I would use the full solitary grove opening.

Likewise, I find it very useful to practice other kinds of bardic arts, such as my panflute, after performing the SOP. In both cases, the SOP balances the energetics of the Druid and the space, and allows for a kind of intense focus on the work at hand. The differences in crafting within an open grove and without one I have found to be quite substantial.

Conclusion

The SOP has become my go-to practice, not only for necessary daily magical protection and as part of my ongoing AODA practice, but also in other meaningful ways. I have found that the more I embraced this practice as a core of my Druidic path, the more benefits and blessings it manifested in my life. The SOP is a versatile ritual that can be used for a variety of circumstances and places.

References

Greer, J. M. (2007). *The Druid magic handbook*. San Francisco: Weiser Books.

Greer, J. M. (2009, April 28). Response to "Coping energy, if you would?" [Electronic mailing list message]. AODA Public. Retrieved from
https://groups.yahoo.com/neo/groups/AODA_Public/conversations/messages/21604

Gilbert, J., & Greer, J. M. (2003). The sphere of protection and elemental working. Ancient Order of Druids in America. Retrieved from
http://aoda.org/Articles/The_Sphere_of_Protection.html

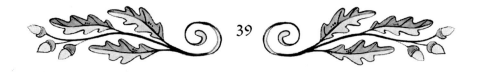

Swordplay in the Sphere of Protection

Tracy Glomski

Tracy Glomski is the present Grand Pendragon of the Ancient Order of Druids in America. A student of the Dolmen Arch course taught by John Michael Greer, she is currently pursuing Gradd yr Athroniwr, Grade of the Philosophizer. Chronically suspicious of such adages as "the pen is mightier than the sword," Tracy hedges her bets by practicing both.

The Grove sword performs a twofold function in the public rituals of the Ancient Order of Druids in America. During the opening ceremonies, the sword is partially unsheathed and then resheathed at each of the four directions as a declaration of peace. During the closing ceremonies, it is presented as the likeness of Excalibur for a pledge of service to the living Earth (Greer, 2006, 2011).

These are both sublime, elegant applications. Still, there is plenty of room for the development of a more elaborate praxis of sword work in the Druid Revival tradition.

I am particularly excited about the prospects of bringing the sword into the Sphere of Protection, the daily ritual performed by members of the AODA. In this article, I share one example of a Sphere of Protection variation that has worked well for me, which seamlessly integrates the sword into the Three Cauldrons exercise of *The Druid Magic Handbook* (Greer, 2007, pp. 193–199). This method is not quite beginner level, in the sense that it assumes the practitioner is already conducting the Sphere of Protection regularly and has also begun to explore the Three Cauldrons, the very first part of the Inner Grail working that is detailed in *The Druid Magic Handbook*. As soon as those prerequisites have been met, however, nothing else is required except the sword itself. Because the sword is moved in a slow and deliberate fashion, no prior training in sword work is necessary. It is simply important to handle the sword with the same respect that is appropriate for all types of sharp implements. To minimize distractions, I recommend practicing in the most private and least cluttered space available.

While this ritual could potentially be adapted with varying degrees of success for swords of different types, it is designed specifically for a medieval long sword. This style of sword features a straight, double-edged blade and a cruciform hilt permitting two-handed use (figure 1).

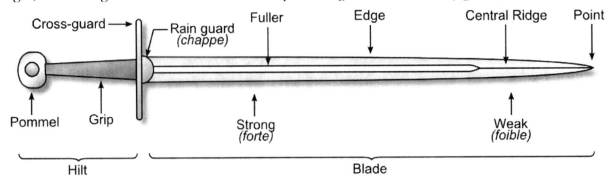

Figure 1: For this ritual, the key parts of the medieval long sword will be the forte, foible, and point of the blade, and the pommel and cross-guard of the hilt. The two arms of the cross-guard are also known as the quillons, pronounced kee-YAWN. (Aeonx, 2010)

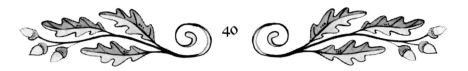

For those who have not had the opportunity to study historical European swordsmanship, as was the case for me when I began this work in 2012, two aspects of this ritual call for further explanation. The first aspect concerns the set of principles invoked in the Elemental Cross. The Elemental Cross is the opening segment of the Sphere of Protection, and its purpose is to establish an orientation within a structure consisting of a balanced array of four cosmic expressions. Each ritualist may freely choose the details of the four expressions. Customarily, the ritualist names deities, spiritual forces, natural phenomena, saints, animal powers, magical symbols, or other similar qualities (Greer, 2007). My own sword form draws upon a quartet of virtues that resemble the cardinal virtues derived from Plato's work and assimilated into Christianity. They are not identical, however. Two of the cardinal virtues—prudence and fortitude—are retained, whereas celerity and audacity replace the remaining two.

The source of this unusual configuration is the sette spade, or "seven swords," illustration featured in *The Flower of Battle*, a treatise composed in the first decade of the fifteenth century by the Italian diplomat and master-at-arms Fiore de'i Liberi. The sette spade appears as a full-page illumination in the *Flos Duellatorum*, the Pisani Dossi manuscript of 1410, which is presently in the care of a private collector. A similar diagram graces another edition of the work, *Fior di Battaglia*, in the holdings of the J. Paul Getty Museum in Los Angeles, California. One other version, unfortunately water damaged, was recognized only a few years ago, tucked away in the Bibliothèque Nationale de France under the title *Florius de Arte Luctandi* (Mondschein, 2008).

I first began to study the sette spade around the time I became an apprentice in the AODA. That accomplishment was an event to celebrate, and I bought myself the gift of a ceremonial sword. The legends of King Arthur play a significant role in the Druid Revival tradition, so the medieval long sword that I acquired is, in many ways, the classic choice for Grove ritual. But I had never previously owned a sword of this or any type. I became curious about how they work. The sette spade was among the first information I encountered. It captivated me right away, with its symbolic depiction of Fiore's four virtues, so neatly arranged in a distinctive cruciform pattern (figure 2).

Through meditation on the sette spade, I have come to believe that the four virtues were each placed with deliberate care. The student in their midst is in a vulnerable position, with the points of the seven swords directed at him. Yet aid is available in the form of four animals wearing collars of gold—the same gilt that adorns the instructor's crown elsewhere in the manuscript—which means they are the properties of mastery. Prudence, the pivotal virtue through which appropriateness of action is determined, is located at the head. Fortitude, the grounded yet upright form of strength that endures all burdens, is at the feet. Celerity, the capacity of swiftness in movement, is at the right side, the dominant side for the majority of practitioners. Audacity, the unabashed display of courage, is at the left side, the same anatomical side as the heart. In my view, prudence serves as the foremost moral virtue at the top position, ideally preventing trouble in the first place, while the three virtues below are excellent and necessary skills to have in a fight. It is also worth noting, however, that the prologue of the *Flos Duellatorum* includes a poem that emphasizes, "Audacity is the virtue that makes this art" (Fiore de'i Liberi, n.d.). There is an interesting tension between that statement, which appears to exalt audacity as the most essential virtue, and Fiore's placement of audacity at the side of the body that is, for the majority of people, the weaker side. I leave further reflection upon that matter as an exercise for the reader. Left-handers might wish to experiment with flipping the

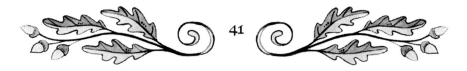

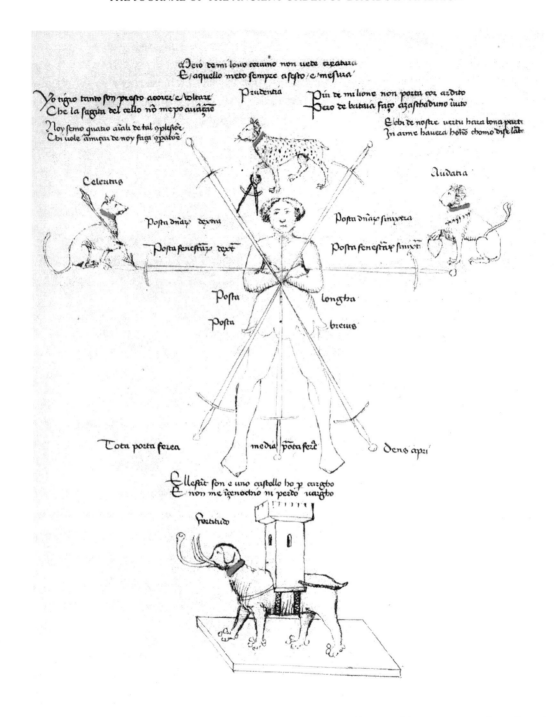

Figure 2: The sette spade (seven swords) diagram incorporates four emblems representing the virtues of swordsmanship. Shown clockwise from top: a lynx and compass for prudence, a lion and heart for audacity, an elephant and castle for fortitude, and a tiger and arrow for celerity. The original Pisani Dossi manuscript vanished during World War II and did not resurface again until 2005. This reproduction is from a popular facsimile (Novati, 1902).

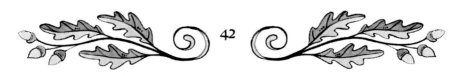

positions of celerity and audacity in the Elemental Cross to determine what feels most natural. Otherwise, I would suggest that it makes a great deal of sense to invoke the virtues in the order presented.

The other aspect that might be unfamiliar to novices is the family of guards, or readiness postures, now blended into the second section of the Sphere of Protection. This segment, the Calling of the Elements, acknowledges seven elements of Nature: the four material elements of classical Greek thought—Air, Fire, Water, and Earth—and three spiritual elements, which are designated Spirit Below, Spirit Above, and Spirit Within.

The four guards, or vier leger, were the core stances of vigilance taught by Johannes Liechtenauer (figure 3). Liechtenauer was an immensely influential master of German swordsmanship, and yet no direct record of his life has survived. Currently, the best guess among scholars of medieval manuscripts is that Liechtenauer taught in the 1300s. He concealed his method in cryptic verses, which served as mnemonic aids for the initiated. If not for the elucidating commentaries of his admirers, his work undoubtedly would have been lost to students today (Johannes Liechtenauer, n.d.). My personal experience with the four guards is that they are not particularly difficult to learn, at a competency acceptable for ritual work, through simple observation and practice of the poses as they appear in reputable sources. During my own self-teaching process, I found it helpful to examine both photographs (Clements, 2004) and illustrations (Lindholm & Svärd, 2003).

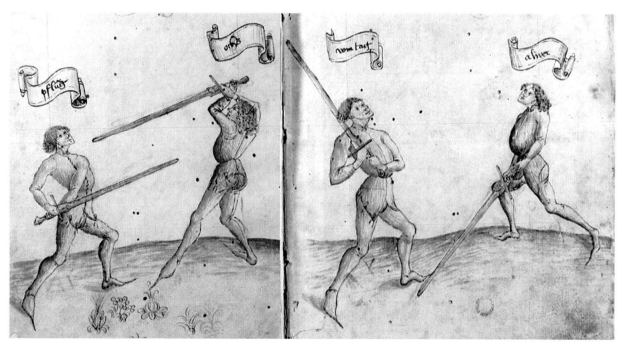

Figure 3: Several historical sources have transmitted the four guards, including Codex 44 A 8, a manual compiled by Peter von Danzig in the 15th century. Shown in pairs from left to right: Pflug (plow) and Ochs (ox) (Danzig, 1452a), and vom Tag (from the roof) and Alber (fool) (Danzig, 1452b).

I was able to discern one-to-one correspondences between the guards and the classical elements by feel alone. One of the interesting effects of a daily practice of the Sphere of Protection is that it tends to heighten the intuitive awareness of such associations. But a little additional research soon

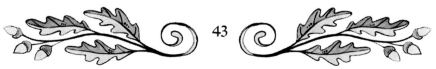

revealed that these relationships had already been derived in a more expert manner. In his essay "Hot, Wet, Cold, and Dry: The Four Guards," Christian Henry Tobler (2010) analyzed the connections between the height of each Liechtenauer guard and its "temperature," and between the openness of these stances and "humidity." Similar ideas also appeared in an earlier, briefer piece by Catriona McDonald (2008), a member of the Order of Bards, Ovates and Druids. Their conclusions and my perceptions agree: Ochs corresponds most naturally with Air (hot, wet), vom Tag with Fire (hot, dry), Pflug with Water (cold, wet), and Alber with Earth (cold, dry).

Having said that, I would consider the set of four guards, and the sword-oriented invocations that accompany them, to be entirely optional for inclusion in the ritual that follows. I personally enjoy doing the stances, because I have discovered that they enhance my feel for the sword as an integral extension of my mind/will/heart/body. The sword is the instrument that symbolizes and amplifies my commitment to serve a higher good and a broader purpose. I have also repeatedly tested the ritual without the four guards, however, and it still feels powerful to me to simply trace the symbols with the sword and to visualize colored light moving through it in the manner that I describe below. The sword work instructions are right-handed—lefties who perform the guards might prefer to do them on the left side, stepping back with the left foot instead of the right.

Part 1: The Elemental Cross

(To begin, hold the sword by the grip in the left hand, thumb uppermost, so the sword points down with the cross-guard positioned in front of the solar plexus. Face east. Imagine the Sun overhead at the zenith.)

(Extend the index and middle fingers of the right hand together, and point to the Sun above. In the space between the Sun and your body, picture a lynx with a compass, representing foresight. Trace a ray of light from the Sun, through the lynx, to the forehead. Touch the fingertips to the forehead and say:)

Prudentia. (pronounced proo-DEN-shee-ə).

(Visualize a sphere of light shining like a star within your head. Imagine this light reflected in the pommel of the sword. Then continue tracing the ray down to the solar plexus. Touch your fingers to that spot and visualize a second sphere of light there. Say:)

Fortitudo. (pronounced fort-ə-TOOD-oh).

(Visualize the ray of light continuing still further downward, reflected in the blade of the sword as it travels. As it reaches the feet, imagine the ray passing through an elephant bearing a castle on its back, which represents strength. The ray continues onward until it reaches the silver-green ball of fire at the Earth's heart.)

(Bring the hand up from the solar plexus and touch the right shoulder with the fingertips. Imagine a ray shooting out from the solar plexus directly to the right, its reflection visible in the right quillon, and passing through a tiger and arrow representing swiftness, and continuing on as far as the mind's eye can see. Say:)

Celeritas. (pronounced kə-LER-ə-tahs).

(Take the hand to the left shoulder and touch it with the fingertips. Imagine a ray shooting out from the solar plexus directly to the left, its reflection visible in the left quillon, and passing through a lion and heart representing boldness, and continuing on as far as the mind's eye can see. Say:)

Audatia. (pronounced: ow (rhymes with "vow")-DA-shee-ə).

(Place the right hand over the heart. Imagine a pair of rays shooting out from the solar plexus, one traveling infinitely far to the back and the other infinitely far to the front. Say:)

May these Virtues be my virtues, this day and always.

Part 2: The Calling of the Elements

(Continue to face east, take the grip of the sword in both hands, and trace the invoking symbol of Air in yellow light: a large, clockwise circle begun at its topmost point and then a line segment upward. Imagine the circle filled with yellow flame. While doing this, say:)

By the yellow gate of the rushing winds and the hawk of May in the heights of morning, and in the great name HU, I invoke the Air, its gods, its spirits, and its powers.

(Bring the sword inward close to the body, point up and hilt near the abdomen, so the cross-guard rests at the level of the solar plexus. Say:)

May I receive the blessings of Air this day and always, that I may attain Gwynfydd in this life.

(Take three slow, deep breaths. With each inhalation, visualize a beam of yellow light streaming from the circle toward and into the cross-guard of the sword, where it divides and radiates all the way up to the point of the blade and all the way down into the pommel. At the same time, the split beam passes through the cross-guard into the solar plexus, where it proceeds to illuminate the inside of the body with yellow light up to the head and down to the feet. With each exhalation, visualize the light emptying out of the body and sword along the same route, and causing the immediate space around the body to fill with a yellow glow. The radius of this glowing sphere should be equivalent to the maximum physical reach of the sword, if it were to be swept to each side and overhead with fully extended arms. When the third breath is complete, say:)

May the powers of Air inform my mind in the use of this sword.

(Pass the right foot back, indicating readiness to receive with strength, and swivel the sword up into the guard of Ochs, the ox. Take three slow, deep breaths. With each inhalation, visualize the yellow glow around the body entering the forte of the blade and passing from the sword into the body itself. With each exhalation, send the glow back out of the body through the foible of the blade.)

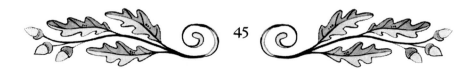

(When the third breath is complete, step out of Ochs into a neutral stance, with the knees slightly bent and the feet comfortably apart. Use the sword to trace the banishing symbol of Air in yellow light: the circle from its topmost point and in the counterclockwise direction, followed by the upward line segment. While doing this, say:)

I thank the Air for its gifts. And with the help of the powers of Air, I banish from within me and around me and from all my doings all unbalanced manifestations of Air. I banish them far away from me.

(Picture a brisk wind or friendly cyclone sweeping up the unbalanced manifestations and dispersing them harmlessly throughout the atmosphere. Lower the sword, cradling the quillons in the hands so the point hangs a few inches off the ground. Pivot one-quarter turn to the right.)

(Facing south, trace the invoking symbol of Fire in red light: a large, clockwise, upward-pointing triangle begun at its topmost point. Imagine the triangle filled with red flame. While doing this, say:)

By the red gate of the bright flames and the white stag in the summer greenwood, and in the great name SUL, I invoke the Fire, its gods, its spirits, and its powers.

(Bring the sword inward close to the body, point up and hilt near the abdomen, so the cross-guard rests at the level of the solar plexus. Say:)

May I receive the blessings of Fire this day and always, that I may attain Gwynfydd in this life.

(Take three slow, deep breaths. With each inhalation, visualize a beam of red light streaming from the triangle toward the cross-guard of the sword, then radiating throughout the sword and the body. With each exhalation, visualize the light emptying into the immediate space around the body, filling it with a red glow. When the third breath is complete, say:)

May the powers of Fire govern my will in the use of this sword.

(Pass the right foot back, and swing the sword up into the guard of vom Tag, "from the roof." Take three slow, deep breaths. With each inhalation, visualize the red glow around the body entering the forte of the blade and passing from the sword into the body itself. With each exhalation, send the glow back out of the body through the foible of the blade.)

(When the third breath is complete, step out of vom Tag. Use the sword to trace the banishing symbol of Fire in red light: the triangle from its topmost point and in the counterclockwise direction. While doing this, say:)

I thank the Fire for its gifts. And with the help of the powers of Fire, I banish from within me and around me and from all my doings all unbalanced manifestations of Fire. I banish them far away from me.

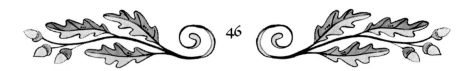

(Picture a lively bonfire reducing the unbalanced manifestations to ashes that float harmlessly away on thermal currents. Lower the sword, cradling the quillons in the hands so the point hangs a few inches off the ground. Pivot one-quarter turn to the right.)

(Facing west, trace the invoking symbol of Water in blue light: a large, clockwise, downward-pointing triangle begun at its bottommost point. Imagine the triangle filled with blue flame. While doing this, say:)

By the blue gate of the mighty waters and the salmon of wisdom in the sacred pool, and in the great name ESUS, I invoke the Water, its gods, its spirits, and its powers.

(Bring the sword inward close to the body, point up and hilt near the abdomen, so the cross-guard rests at the level of the solar plexus. Say:)

May I receive the blessings of Water this day and always, that I may attain Gwynfydd in this life.

(Take three slow, deep breaths. With each inhalation, visualize a beam of blue light streaming from the triangle toward the cross-guard of the sword, then radiating throughout the sword and the body. With each exhalation, visualize the light emptying into the immediate space around the body, filling it with a blue glow. When the third breath is complete, say:)

May the powers of Water guide my heart in the use of this sword.

(Pass the right foot back, and shift the sword down and to the right into the guard of Pflug, the plow. Take three slow, deep breaths. With each inhalation, visualize the blue glow around the body entering the forte of the blade and passing from the sword into the body itself. With each exhalation, send the glow back out of the body through the foible of the blade.)

(When the third breath is complete, step out of Pflug. Use the sword to trace the banishing symbol of Water in blue light: the triangle from its bottommost point and in the counterclockwise direction. While doing this, say:)

I thank the Water for its gifts. And with the help of the powers of Water, I banish from within me and around me and from all my doings all unbalanced manifestations of Water. I banish them far away from me.

(Picture an outgoing tide carrying the unbalanced manifestations deep into the ocean, where they harmlessly dissolve. Lower the sword, cradling the quillons in the hands so the point hangs a few inches off the ground. Pivot one-quarter turn to the right.)

(Facing north, trace the invoking symbol of Earth in green light: a large, clockwise circle begun at its bottommost point and then a line segment downward. Imagine the circle filled with green flame. While doing this, say:)

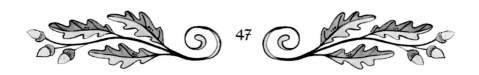

By the green gate of the tall stones and the great bear who guards the starry heavens, and in the great name ELEN, I invoke the Earth, its gods, its spirits, and its powers.

(Bring the sword inward close to the body, point up and hilt near the abdomen, so the cross-guard rests at the level of the solar plexus. Say:)

May I receive the blessings of Earth this day and always, that I may attain Gwynfydd in this life.

(Take three slow, deep breaths. With each inhalation, visualize a beam of green light streaming from the circle toward the cross-guard of the sword, then radiating throughout the sword and the body. With each exhalation, visualize the light emptying into the immediate space around the body, filling it with a green glow. When the third breath is complete, say:)

May the powers of Earth fortify my body in the use of this sword.

(Pass the right foot back, and angle the sword down into the guard of Alber, the fool. Take three slow, deep breaths. With each inhalation, visualize the green glow around the body entering the forte of the blade and passing from the sword into the body itself. With each exhalation, send the glow back out of the body through the foible of the blade.)

(When the third breath is complete, step out of Alber. Use the sword to trace the banishing symbol of Earth in green light: the circle from its bottommost point and in the counterclockwise direction, followed by the downward line segment. While doing this, say:)

I thank the Earth for its gifts. And with the help of the powers of Earth, I banish from within me and around me and from all my doings all unbalanced manifestations of Earth. I banish them far away from me.

(Picture the unbalanced manifestations disappearing into a barrow, where the microfauna of the soil harmlessly digest them. Lower the sword, cradling the quillons in the hands so the point hangs a few inches off the ground. Pivot one-quarter turn to the right.)

(Facing east, take the grip of the downward-pointing sword in both hands, and trace the invoking symbol of Spirit Below: a clockwise circle in orange light and filled with orange flame, near the ground immediately in front of the feet. While doing this, say:)

By the bright heart of the Earth Mother, and in the great name CED, I invoke Spirit Below, its gods, its spirits, and its powers.

(Continue to hold the sword in both hands, with the pommel resting at the lower abdomen near the cauldron of the Earth and the point directed toward the center of the circle drawn for Spirit Below. Say:)

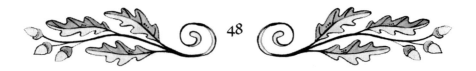

May a ray of the telluric current ascend into me this day and always. May the cauldron of the Earth be filled within me.

(Take three slow, deep breaths. With each inhalation, visualize sparkling silver light of the telluric current ascending through the soles of the feet, up the legs, and into the cauldron of the Earth. With each exhalation, visualize a silvery green glow emanating from the cauldron, through the pommel, and into the sphere that would be defined by the longest reach of the sword. After the third breath, and with the cauldron now full, say:)

I thank Spirit Below for its gifts.

(Lift the sword and trace the invoking symbol of Spirit Above: a clockwise circle in purple light and filled with purple flame, overhead and aligned above the orange circle. While doing this, say:)

By the Sun in its glory, the father of light, and in the great name CELI, I invoke Spirit Above, its gods, its spirits, and its powers.

(Reorient the sword to point downward, shifting the hands so that they cup the quillons with the fingertips directed toward the sword. The cross-guard should rest roughly level with the solar plexus, and the pommel should be at the chest near the cauldron of the Sun. Say:)

May a ray of the solar current descend into me this day and always. May the cauldron of the Sun be filled within me.

(Take three slow, deep breaths. With each inhalation, visualize gleaming golden light of the solar current descending to the level of the cross-guard, then through the solar plexus, and up into the cauldron of the Sun. With each exhalation, visualize a sunny yellow glow emanating from the cauldron, through the pommel, and into the sphere that would be defined by the longest reach of the sword. After the third breath, and with the cauldron now full, say:)

I thank Spirit Above for its gifts.

(Raise the sword so the pommel is level with the forehead, shifting the hands so they cup the quillons with the fingertips directed away from the sword. The point of the sword should hang directly over the center of the circle that was drawn for Spirit Below. Say:)

By the six powers here invoked and here present, and by the grand word by which the worlds were made, AWEN, I invoke Spirit Within.

(Draw the sword in closer to the body, so the pommel is nearly resting on the forehead at the cauldron of the Moon. Say:)

May the lunar current be born within me this day and always. May the cauldron of the Moon be filled within me.

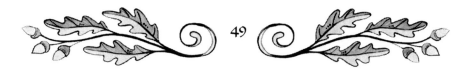

(Take three slow, deep breaths. With each inhalation, visualize silver light streaming up from the cauldron of the Earth and golden light streaming up from the cauldron of the Sun, and combining at the cauldron of the Moon to fill it with white light of unmatched purity. With each exhalation, visualize a clean white glow radiating from the cauldron, through the pommel, and into the sphere that would be defined by the longest reach of the sword. After the third breath, with the cauldron now full, say:)

I thank all the Powers for their blessings.

Part 3: The Circulation of Light

(Visualize a drop of white light descending from the cauldron of the Moon to the solar plexus. As it falls, lower the sword along with it, rotating the hands so they once again cup the quillons with fingertips pointing toward the sword. When the pommel reaches the level of the solar plexus, stop and hold the sword there. Imagine that the drop of lunar current is lighting up the solar plexus, and that this white glow now travels outward in all directions, passing through the pommel and into the sphere that would be defined by the longest reach of the sword, and perhaps beyond that to an even larger sphere if so desired. The surface of this sphere is composed of three interpenetrating spheres that can be spun in independent directions. Say:)

May I continue to be centered . . .

(Spin the first sphere in such a way that a point on the sphere directly overhead would rotate down past the front side of the body, under the feet, and up past the back side of the body to the starting position. Continue to spin it in that direction, faster and faster, until it moves so fast it becomes solid. Say:)

. . . and protected . . .

(Spin the second sphere in such a way that a point on the sphere directly to the left side of the body would rotate across the front side of the body to the right, then from right to left across the back side of the body. Continue to spin it in that direction, faster and faster, until it moves so fast it becomes solid. Say:)

. . . in the service of a higher good.

(Spin the third sphere in such a way that a point on the sphere directly overhead would rotate down past the right side of the body, under the feet, and up past the left side of the body to the starting position. Continue to spin it in that direction, faster and faster, until it moves so fast it becomes solid. The ritual is now complete.)

Conclusion

So, this ritual is obviously rather colorful—a good workout for the muscles of visualization—but beyond that, what purpose does it serve?

One requirement for apprentices in the AODA study program is to conduct the solitary form of the Grove opening and closing ceremonies at least once per week. By shifting the sword into daily work, I have experienced a reinforced cognizance of the oath of the closing ceremony: "By the

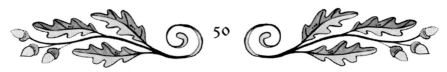

Sword of Swords, I pledge my faithful service to the living Earth, our home and mother." I have noticed a general strengthening of resolve in that direction. For example, I recall that as recently as two years ago, whenever the outdoor temperature fell below 20°F, I would be tempted to drive the mile to work instead of walking. This past winter, when the mercury often dropped considerably lower, I kept walking, even if it was as cold as −10°F. I seem to have developed something like an indifference to the cold. This was a wholly unanticipated effect. I do often find myself thinking about the sword, though, as I walk. The process of routinely handling the sword seems to have brought about a subtle yet significant shift in my self-definition. I feel a mite tougher. I am more ready and willing to take the actions that seem, to me, to be right. Or, as one of my clients observed, in a nice compliment on a frigid day: "In certain circles, Tracy, you would be considered a badass."

Still, the method I have described here is intended as only one possible example. I would be tickled if others would run with these ideas, taking them in different directions, each according to individual Awen. I envision the creation of many new forms of the Sphere of Protection, unlike mine or any other.

To anyone who chooses to tackle that, here are my wishes for you: Have fun. Stay sharp. Be audacious.

References

Aeonx. (2010). Sword parts no scabbard. Retrieved December 24, 2013, from Wikimedia Commons: http://commons.wikimedia.org/wiki/File:Sword_parts_no_scabbard.PNG

Clements, J. (2004). The basic guards of medieval longsword. Retrieved from http://www.thearma.org/essays/StancesIntro.htm

Danzig, P. (1452a). MS 44 A 8 1v. Retrieved December 24, 2013, from Wikimedia Commons: http://commons.wikimedia.org/wiki/File:MS_44_A_8_1v.jpg

Danzig, P. (1452b). MS 44 A 8 2r. Retrieved December 24, 2013, from Wikimedia Commons: http://commons.wikimedia.org/wiki/File:MS_44_A_8_2r.jpg

Fiore de'i Liberi. (n.d.). Retrieved February 7, 2014, from the Historical European Martial Arts Alliance Wiki: http://www.wiktenauer.com/wiki/Fiore_de%27i_Liberi

Greer, J. M. (2006). *The Druidry handbook: Spiritual practice rooted in the living earth.* San Francisco: Weiser.

Greer, J. M. (2007). *The Druid magic handbook: Ritual magic rooted in the living earth.* San Francisco: Weiser.

Greer, J. M. (2011). *The Druid grove handbook: A guide to ritual in the Ancient Order of Druids in America.* Everett, WA: Starseed.

Johannes Liechtenauer. (n.d.). Retrieved February 7, 2014, from the Historical European Martial Arts Alliance Wiki: http://www.wiktenauer.com/wiki/Johannes_Liechtenauer

Lindholm, D., & Svärd, P. (2003). *Sigmund Ringeck's knightly art of the longsword.* Boulder, CO: Paladin Press.

Mondschein, K. (2008). Notes on Bibliothèque Nationale de France MS Lat. 11269. Retrieved from http://historicalfencing.org/papers/Mondschein%20-%20Fiore%20description.pdf

McDonald, C. (2008). Elemental guards. Retrieved from http://www.selohaar.org/Vortex/vElementalGuards.htm

Novati, F. (1902). Pisani Dossi Ms. 16r. Retrieved December 24, 2013, from Wikimedia Commons: http://commons.wikimedia.org/wiki/File:Pisani_Dossi_Ms._16r.jpg

Tobler, C. H. (2010). *In Saint George's name: An anthology of medieval German fighting arts.* Wheaton, IL: Freelance Academy Press.

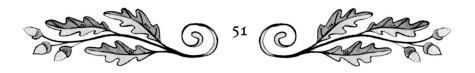

Devotional Practice

Sara Greer

Sara Greer is the Archdruid of the West in AODA, and the preceptor of the clergy training program in the GCC. She has been a Druid for more than twenty years and a polytheist for as long as she can remember. She lives in the hills of northern Appalachia with her husband, a lot of books, and a large stash of craft supplies.

Devotional practice is a hot topic in several religious communities right now, and is a perennial favorite among the questions that land in my inbox as preceptor of the clergy training program for the Gnostic Celtic Church and an Archdruid of AODA. Many of the people who email me want a deeper relationship with their gods, spirits, or ancestors, and have no idea of what to do or where to start in order to achieve that. They tend to have the same three questions: What is devotional practice? Why should I do it? How do I do it?

What is devotional practice, and what's the point of it? Devotional practice is a group of actions that focus on the gods, spirits, and ancestors. Common forms of devotional practice include prayer, offerings, and the creation and maintenance of shrines or altars. Why engage in devotional practice? I'm sure a gathering of devotional practitioners could come up with a dozen or more good reasons, but the most common ones I've seen discussed involve creating, building, or maintaining a relationship with the gods, spirits, and ancestors. The experience of devotional practitioners is that their devotional practices help build relationships with these beings and help develop or deepen their inner spiritual and religious lives also. Creating and tending an altar or shrine and engaging in regular offerings and prayer often have the effect of bringing your awareness and your daily life closer to a focus on the gods, spirits, and ancestors.

Devotional practice has another side when it comes to relationships, too. In any relationship, it's a good idea to express your feelings, to do things to indicate that you love and value the object of your affections. Devotional practice fills this role in a relationship with the gods, spirits, and ancestors. Prayer, offerings, and votive objects serve to express your love, devotion, and gratitude, among other things. It's the religious equivalent of giving your loved ones birthday gifts, taking them out to dinner, calling or texting them to say hello, and sending them emails or postcards when you go out of town. For some people, depending on the details of their beliefs, devotional practice also benefits the gods, spirits, and ancestors in various ways; research on the traditional beliefs of the appropriate cultures will provide more details relevant to specific deities.

How do you engage in devotional practice? Traditions vary somewhat on the details, but the heart of daily devotional religious practice for many traditions lies in two elements: creating, tending, and maintaining one or more shrines or altars, and making offerings. Prayer may be a part of either or both, as I discuss in more detail below. The shrines or altars create a location for you to focus on, a home for the gods, spirits, and ancestors, and a place to make offerings. Offerings serve as gifts, demonstrations of affection, gratitude, or commitment, and ways to engage in the virtue of hospitality and the principle of *do ut des* (reciprocity of giving). This article provides a basic introduction to core devotional practices—how to make and tend shrines and altars, and how to make offerings of different kinds—so that readers who are interested in these practices but have no

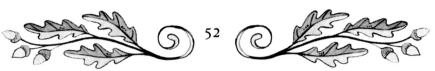

idea of where to start can pick up some ideas. I also include a section on devotional practices and the challenges of travel, for those readers who may need or want to travel and want to continue devotional practices during their journey.

Shrines and Altars

What constitutes a shrine or an altar, and what's the difference between them? Opinions and definitions vary a bit, but the basic rules of thumb that I learned as a trainee priestess define a shrine as a place where deities, spirits, and ancestors are honored and memorialized, and an altar as a place where religious or magical ritual is carried out. It's possible to use the same table or other flat surface as both a shrine and an altar, or you can separate them. Many people who spend a lot of time working with the gods, spirits, and ancestors have multiple shrines or altars in their living spaces, depending on their needs, and a lot of us also manage to make small shrines in our workplaces as well. Often, workplace shrines need to look like they're decorations rather than devotional spaces, which can be achieved by using objects that have special associations for you but look ordinary to your coworkers.

Shrines and altars need not be permanent, but if you're going to do devotional work regularly it's a good idea to find or create a space where you can do at least basic practices every day. Having a stable location makes it easier to get daily devotional practices done, especially if you tend to be short on time, because you can leave the basic setup in place; it takes more time and energy to have to set it up and take it down over and over again. Part or all of a tabletop or desktop, the top of a nightstand, the top of a bookcase or file cabinet, or the top of a trunk or chest of drawers make good spots and are readily available in many homes or offices. A fairly small space can be plenty for basic daily prayer and offerings; if need be I can make do with an altar space about six inches on a side, for instance, and when I'm traveling with my tiny portable altar, an area about four inches square is plenty big enough. At my office, a space about three inches square serves to hold a collection of small objects that makes up a covert shrine. However, if you have a larger space available by all means use it. My main altar is roughly a foot square, and my shrines range in size from about eight by nine inches to an entire six-inch-wide, three-foot-long shelf.

Decorating a shrine involves assembling a collection of meaningful objects and arranging them on a tabletop, shelf, TV tray, or other location. A flat surface is the most common available space in most houses, apartments, or offices. I've seen some very creative shrines that made use of other kinds of spaces based on what was available, though, so don't be afraid to experiment. A shadowbox, a knickknack shelf, a pocket vase hung on the wall, an appliquéd felt wall hanging decorated with pendants of shells, carved stones, and animal-shaped beads: all of these could be, and have been, used as shrines.

Shrines may contain any or all of the following items, depending on your needs and preferences: framed or unframed photographs, paintings, prints, or other pieces of representational art, which can be propped up on a shelf or tabletop or hung on the wall above or behind it; statues, figurines, dolls, or other three-dimensional images of gods, spirits, or ancestors; votive objects, such as stones, shells, flowers, roots, jewelry, statues, prayer beads, prayer cards, vases, bowls, cups, and so on; memorial objects, such as something that once belonged to or was made by an ancestor; and various other things as the shrine's creator sees fit.

To give a few examples, one of my shrines includes statues of five deities, carved figures of

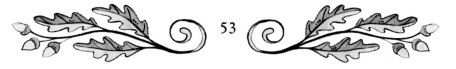

various kinds representing nature spirits who are important to my work, and several votive objects—pieces of jewelry, small carvings, special stones, and strands of prayer beads—dedicated to various deities. Another of my shrines, dedicated solely to nature spirits, contains an animal figurine and a small collection of natural objects. A covert shrine I once had at my desk at work in an accounting office consisted of a small ceramic dish containing a nut in the shell, a few small dried flowers, and a pebble; behind the dish I had a miniature glass bottle full of beach sand and tiny seashells, and a little carved figurine of an animal. Each of these items had specific religious associations and significance for me, but nobody in the office realized it was anything other than a decorative display.

Altars can be established on any suitable flat surface, permanent or temporary. I use the tops of bookshelves or small tables for permanent altars, and folding wooden TV trays or the top of a hotel room chest of drawers for temporary ones. Make sure the altar is stable before you use it, because you don't want to have open water vessels, dishes of food, goblets of liquid, burning incense, or anything with open flames set out on top of an object that may fall or tip over.

Altar furnishings often are a bit more spare than shrine decorations; a working altar shouldn't be too cluttered because clutter gets in the way. However, that said, individual tastes and needs may vary, sometimes quite a lot. Altars may contain lamps, candleholders, or incense burners; plates, saucers, bowls, cups, goblets, jars, or other offering vessels; religious images; and formally dedicated religious or magical tools used in rituals, such as knives, wands, cups, votive jewelry or prayer beads, divinatory sets, and so on.

Again, to give a few examples, my main altar, which is permanent, contains offering vessels that I use daily, which are always kept on the altar. It also contains a rotating collection of votive and ritual objects that are relevant to the season, to specific deities I'm doing intensive work with, or to particular rituals I'm getting ready to do. These objects change at regular or irregular intervals, depending on why they're on the altar and when their immediate purpose is fulfilled. Another permanent altar contains offering vessels for weekly use, and a small collection of votive objects that rarely change. A temporary altar I set up on special occasions for specific rituals contains candles, incense, a water vessel, and symbols relevant to the ritual. Items from my temporary altar are stored when not in use, since the altar is set up on a small table that has other uses between rituals.

Once set up and decorated, the shrines and altars need to be tended. How often you tend them depends a great deal on where you make your offerings and where you do your rituals. I make formal offerings each day at my main altar, so I tend it daily. I offer fresh water, fire, incense or sweet herbs, and prayer. I begin by washing the water bowl, drying the outside of it, and filling it with fresh water. Then I select the incense and put a stick of it in the burner, if I'm going to offer incense, or select the sweet herbs and place them in an offering dish if I'm going to offer herbs. (I discuss the offerings, including sweet herbs, in more detail below, including what sweet herbs are commonly used and how and when to dispose of perishable offerings.) I light the tea light that's already in my altar candleholder, light the incense, and make my prayers. Later, after the candle and incense have burned out, I empty the water bowl, wash and dry it, and place it back on the altar. I remove the tea light cup from the candleholder and place it in a bag of others to be refilled, and place a fresh candle in the holder before replacing the holder on the altar. Finally, I clean the incense burner if necessary, and then the daily portion of tending my altar is complete.

Every couple of weeks or once a month, I clean the entire altar by taking everything off it, dusting and cleaning the surface, and then returning the items one by one, dusting or cleaning them

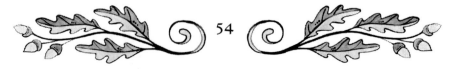

as necessary. At this time I also remove items that no longer need to be on the altar, and add anything that may not have been on it already but that now needs to be. I tend my shrines the same way. I always make sure that my offering vessels are quite clean before I use them, regardless of the type of offering I'm going to use them to receive.

Offerings

Even before you've set up an altar or shrine, you can make offerings. Offerings may consist of food and drink; water (which may be mixed into or offered separately from and in addition to another beverage, such as wine or milk); fire or light; incense, perfumes, or sweet herbs; prayers; creative works such as poetry, music, artworks, and crafted items; devotional or votive objects you've found, made, or purchased; and various actions or activities, including acts of charity and hospitality. Any or all of these things may be given to, given in the name of, or performed in the name of or in the honor of one or more gods, spirits, and ancestors.

Food and Drink

The details of what to offer to whom vary quite a bit from one culture and tradition to another, but there are some underlying principles that apply fairly widely.

When offering food to nature spirits, faeries, and similar beings, it's most common to leave the offering in a suitable location—on a flat rock, under a tree, on a dish on your back step—and the offering is not shared, that is, you shouldn't eat or drink what you put out for the offering. As to what you should offer, it's usually best to check the preferences of the spirits in question if you're able. If not, most spirits have preferences that are recorded in folklore or known to experienced practitioners.

For example, faeries are said to be very fond of bread, milk, and sweet foods, and to reject meat or foods made with meat juices, gravy, or blood (such as blood sausage or blood puddings). The faeries I leave offerings for love dairy products, sweets, fruits, and vegetables, but don't want meat or dishes that contain meat products, and don't want eggs except when baked or otherwise cooked into foods such as cookies, pancakes, or cake. They like it if I compost food offerings I've left for them once they're finished, when those are compatible with my compost heap. However, items such as cookies, corn sticks, and buttered bread aren't good for a compost heap because of the fats they contain, so those I put in the garbage or leave out for animals to eat. (Our local opossums and raccoons are happy to oblige, and the faeries are equally satisfied for their treats to go to feed animals or to feed compost heap insects and bacteria.)

Nature spirits are a much more varied lot, with widely varying tastes, so look to local folklore and folk magic traditions to get some ideas of what to offer. The spirits where I live usually like libations, especially water, and also enjoy it if I offer them a soil-nourishing herbal tea such as comfrey or nettle, or vegetable broth. They also like simple food offerings such as slices of fresh bread, fresh fruit or vegetables, jam, homemade pickles, and sprigs of sweet herbs, but they're not fond of animal products of any description and they don't like added fats: they'd rather have their bread without butter, although they're happy to have it topped with a layer of jam.

Foods and beverage offerings for ancestors are much easier to research. For a remote ancestor, I suggest that you follow cultural norms for their native culture where possible. For a more recent ancestor, especially if you knew them or know something from family stories about what they liked

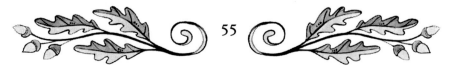

to eat or drink, I've found that it's generally a good choice to offer their favorite foods or a dish that's part of your family tradition. Never consume these offerings yourself: in every culture I've researched, food and beverages left out for the dead are forbidden for the living to consume, and are thrown away afterward. Again, the appropriate traditional cultures are likely to provide information on the details of appropriate disposal, and if not, then in my experience it's fairly safe to bury the offerings or throw them in the garbage.

Another potential food offering for ancestors consists of a dumb supper or an equivalent rite in which the dead are invited to partake of a meal with you, and one or more places are set at the table for them. In some versions of this custom, food is placed on the plates set out for the dead, and the plates set at their places at the table; the living then take portions of food from the serving dishes and eat in silence while the dead are presumed to be consuming their offerings. With that sort of meal, you can eat any leftovers remaining in the serving dishes, but should throw away the food that was actually placed on the plates of the ancestors. Another option is to prepare the food, take a portion of each dish for yourself, and then invite the dead to consume the food that remains in the serving dishes; you then eat your portion while the dead presumably serve themselves as they wish. When this kind of meal is finished, you should throw away all of the food from the serving dishes.

The norms for offerings of food and drink for the gods differ greatly from one culture to another in terms of what to serve, how, and when. If at all possible you should research the culture relevant to the god(s) to whom you want to make offerings, to ensure that both what you offer and how you offer it are acceptable. Crucially, cultures differ a great deal as to whether it's acceptable to either consume the food and drink—in a shared meal similar to the dumb supper, where you take a portion of the food and serve a portion to the god(s), or taking the offering and consuming it yourself after the ritual is finished—or whether you should throw it away. I've found that as a rule, in cultures where it's acceptable to consume the offering, such as the Japanese habit of taking the water, rice, and sake offered at a home shrine and cooking it into a family meal, it's also considered rude or ignorant not to consume the offerings; equally, in cultures where it's considered unacceptable to consume the offerings, consuming them is viewed as rude and perhaps even sacrilegious. This is an issue where it's wise to step carefully, in other words.

The same is true of libations: in some cultures it's considered acceptable and even required to drink a portion of what you pour out onto the earth or serve to the gods upon the altar, and in others it's utterly unacceptable and scandalous to do so. Because customs vary and the wrong choice can be loaded, it's a good idea to check the appropriate cultural traditions. If you worship gods from a culture where we have no record of the traditions, then either seek for an omen of what the gods want you to do (divination is a good method to use), or opt not to consume the offerings and explain in your prayers that you're trying to be polite and avoid wrong behavior. It seems in most cultures to be less offensive to pass up sharing the gods' meal than to share it inappropriately.

Water

A frequent offering on altars, water is almost always an acceptable libation to gods, spirits, and ancestors. In my experience trees benefit from having fresh water poured along their drip lines, bushes and flowers thrive on having their roots watered in appropriate amounts, and animals and faeries enjoy a bowl of fresh clean water.

If you offer water on your altar, first wash the bowl thoroughly as a courtesy and then fill it with

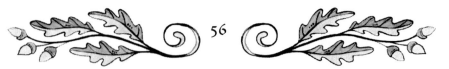

fresh water. When a reasonable amount of time has passed, pour the water out and wash the bowl. Don't let the water get stale, and if you leave the bowl empty between offerings, don't let it get dusty. (If it does get dusty, wash it out before using it again.) In my experience, gods, spirits, and ancestors prefer fresh water, from the tap or from a stream, to bottled water, but if all you can get is bottled water for some reason (say, you're out hiking in the woods with no stream nearby and the only water available is what you carried in with you), that's better than nothing.

Fire and Light

In many cultures, the gods, spirits, and ancestors like offerings of fire. They are still feasible, and a very important form of offering, but they do require you to be aware of and practice the basic principles of fire safety. I'm only going to cover small fire offerings that are suitable for an indoor setting; they have just a few simple (but very important) safety rules. Place any vessels that contain fire offerings on a heatproof, nonflammable surface; a thick cork mat or coaster works well. Watch for anything that might stray across an open flame: tie back curtains or keep the flame well away from them; roll up or pin back the sleeves of your robe; tie your hair back; make sure you know where the ends of your sash or belt are; and keep your jewelry out of the way. Never place an open flame near an open window, especially in windy weather. At all times, be aware where the flame is, how large it is, and how it's behaving. Never leave an open flame unattended.

Candles are an excellent form of fire offering in the modern industrialized world, where hearth fires and coal or wood stoves are no longer the norm. If you have safety concerns, avoid tapers, pillars, or other tall unshielded candles and opt for votive candles or tea lights placed in a symbolically appropriate heat-proof holder. They are relatively safe; they rarely spill or fall over. In a situation where you need the flame to burn longer than an hour or two, a glass-encased novena candle is a good choice. As with votives and tea lights, these candles are relatively safe.

Small oil lamps are also very good for fire offerings, whether you choose a miniature hurricane lamp, one of the modern olive oil lamps consisting of a wick setup in a small glass jar, or a more traditional stone or pottery lamp with a wick. Note that if you use small unglazed pottery oil lamps or lamps carved of a porous stone such as soapstone, oil will gradually leak through the pores of the lamp. Thus it's best to fill them just before use and empty and clean them immediately you're finished with them, or put them on a small saucer to catch and contain the leaking oil.

Fire bowls are also an option; a mixture of small amounts of salt and sugar with Everclear or other high-proof alcohol poured over them and lit makes a lovely and relatively cool fire, and can be used to burn up small flammable offerings such as a prayer paper. Make sure to use a fireproof vessel (a bronze or cast iron quaich or miniature cauldron is good) and to place it on a thick cork mat before lighting the fire. Also be extremely careful to watch yourself and the fire's surroundings for anything that might stray into the edges of the flames, because the flames in a fire bowl flicker, flare, and leap unpredictably. Never leave the room while a fire bowl is burning!

If you can't have open flame for some reason (e.g., you use oxygen, you're staying in a hotel), you can use some other source of light in a ritual that calls for fire. I've seen battery-powered imitation candles, small strings of holiday lights, and miniature Cyalume light sticks used with acceptable results. I've also seen night-lights and small electric lamps (book lights, task lights) used when someone needed to keep a shrine lit for a fixed period of time and was unable to leave a flame burning unattended. You can also, if you choose and if your religious tradition permits, opt to skip

making an offering of fire and focus on something that works better for you.

Incense, Perfumes, and Sweet Herbs

Incense is one of those bog standard offerings found in many cultures. Stick or cone, loose herbs or resin chunks, powders, and so on, are all usable and acceptable. Check the lore of the appropriate traditional culture to find out if anything is known about the specific preferences of your chosen gods or spirits; for ancestors, try to find out both the traditional lore and what they liked, if anything. Practices varied a good deal in traditional cultures, as much with incense as with other offerings. You may find that specific incenses or herbs were used for specific holy days or at certain times of year, or that deities each had their own specific incenses, or that certain formulations were used in the temples at all times.

If you can't handle the smoke (say, you or someone in your household has asthma), or if you can't have anything burning (you're in a hotel room, you or someone in your household uses an oxygen tank, etc.), try placing a few drops of perfume or essential oil in a small dish. A spritz of floral water from a spray bottle or mister also does a nice job of freshening and scenting the air over the altar or shrine. Here again, check traditional lore to find out what herbs were favored by what gods or spirits, and use essential oils or floral waters according to what you find. For ancestors, seek what they enjoyed or what was traditional as an offering to the dead in their culture.

If perfumes or oils don't work for you (perhaps you or someone who shares your living space suffers from perfume allergies or migraines triggered by strong scents), fresh or dried sweet herbs and spices make a nice offering. You have a lot of options here: rose petals; lavender buds; mint leaves; sprigs or leaves of rosemary, sweet marjoram, oregano, or thyme; a small bowl of sweet woodruff or homemade herbal potpourri without added scent; meadowsweet, honeysuckle, or jasmine flowers; a small amount of cinnamon, nutmeg, ginger, or cloves in a saucer or bowl; and so on. Again, check traditional lore or family stories to choose appropriate herbs and spices.

Prayer

Prayer is more or less always acceptable in every culture. As always, check traditions to see what was habitually used. If there's no record, you can experiment with different formats, postures, times of day, days of the week, and themes to see what gets a good response.

Prayers may be offered equally at shrines or altars, or at both if you wish. They may be offered at any time of day or night, silently or aloud, in the form of poetry or chant or song or simply as spoken words. They can be short or long or in between; they can be simple or complex, formal or casual. Prayers can be songs of praise, cries for help, celebrations of a festival, expressions of love and devotion, or records of a god or spirit or ancestor's deeds. They may be repetitive, even mantric, or may contain no repetition. You can use strands of prayer beads to mark your place in the prayer, or pray holding a devotional object such as a figurine, or pray empty-handed. You can wear a shawl or scarf or piece of devotional jewelry to mark out your prayer time, or you can pray in ordinary street clothes, in your bathrobe and PJs, or stark naked. You can recite prayers as you wash the dishes, during your commute to work, or while feeding the cat or making your bed.

Prayers are versatile and always available. If you can't find words, you can simply offer your undivided attention and clear your mind of all thoughts except those of the gods, spirits, or ancestors to whom you are praying. You can reach out in thought or with silent gestures to reinforce

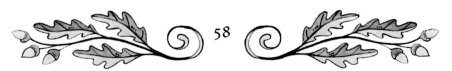

a wordless prayer. You can offer yourself and all that you are in a silent act of devotion, and you'll be heard as clearly as if you'd used the most eloquent of words.

If you feel a need or desire to read the prayers of others, you can find a number of good books of prayers, including books on how to write prayers and devotional anthologies full of prayers dedicated to specific deities. Many religious blogs also post prayers, and some blogs host traditional poetic prayer contests (known as *agon*). Half an hour or an hour spent doing Internet research will yield a lot of useful material.

Poetry

Devotional poetry is almost as versatile a form of offering as prayer, and of course the two can easily be combined. An offering of poetry may be written or performed as a form of prayer, as praise, as a retelling of a myth or legend or family story about the gods, spirits, or ancestors in question, as an expression of love or gratitude or commitment, or for many other reasons. You can write your poem on a piece of paper and burn it to send your words to the gods, spirits, and ancestors; you can recite or sing it; you can print or calligraph it on beautiful paper, frame it, and hang it on the wall over your altar or shrine; you can recite it during an offering ritual, or repeat it silently to yourself whenever you approach your altar or shrine, or use it as a bedtime prayer; you can publish it in a blog post, a magazine, or a devotional anthology; you can write it in your own personal prayer book; you can write a piece of music for it and turn it into a song of devotion.

Many people find it inspirational to study traditional poetic forms, especially those from the cultures from which their deities, spirits, and ancestors came. A range of good books on poetic forms exist, especially those written by actual working poets, and if you want poetic inspiration, time spent reading some may be a good investment.

Music

Music is another readily available form of offering that has been used in many different cultures. If you want to make an offering of music, you can write a piece of music, perform one written by someone else, or play a recording. For ancestor offerings, choose a piece they were especially fond of during their life, or something that reminds you of them. Was your great aunt a flapper who danced to jazz bands? Did Grandma Mabel love Tennessee Ernie Ford? Was Cousin George a classical pianist with a thing for Satie? That gives you some clues to what to select. For nature spirits and faeries, look for pieces of music that depict the natural world, or for tunes and songs associated with faeries or spirits: *Night on Bald Mountain*, Shetland trowie tunes, the *Fingal's Cave Overture*, and such.

For the gods, cast your net wide; any piece that inspires you with feelings of awe or reverence, reminds you of a given deity, or makes you feel connected to a deity, might be a suitable offering. Modern American culture tends to default toward hymn tunes and classical music for religious purposes, but in fact nearly any kind of music can make an appropriate devotional offering if it's relevant to the deity or to the occasion. That said, however, don't ignore classical music or hymn tunes just because they're the default option; they can still be of use or value. The most powerful invocation of the gods I've ever experienced was a skilled opera company's performance of "O Isis und Osiris" from Mozart's *The Magic Flute*. The presence of both deities filled the opera house so completely that for a few minutes I found it difficult to breathe, and the experience left several

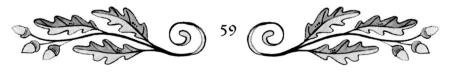

members of my party white and shaken because they had never felt the descent of the gods so strongly before.

Arts and Crafts

All around the world, down through the ages, people from every culture have made artworks and crafts with their hands to offer to the gods. A piece of artwork can be made or purchased and dedicated as a votive offering to gods, spirits, or ancestors. If you yourself are an artist or crafter, then use your talents and skills: paint a portrait of a deity, photograph a beautiful natural scene, sculpt an image of an animal spirit, draw your late grandma as you remember her, whittle a traditional wooden toy the way your great uncle used to, throw a piece of pottery to use as an offering vessel, mold some Fimo into prayer beads, weave a ritual scarf to wear, embroider an image of your patron goddess's favorite flowers onto your altar cloth, sew or quilt an altar cloth, or in whatever other fashion occurs to you, create an original artwork and offer it up. Such items can become permanent or seasonal fixtures on your altar or in your shrine, used to decorate your person or your home, or sold or given to others in honor of or in the name of the deity, spirit, or ancestor for whom they were made.

Devotional Objects

The making of votive (dedicated devotional) offerings is another cross-cultural act of devotion, and it overlaps with the arts and crafts category discussed above. You can find, make, or purchase a wide range of objects that may be dedicated to the gods, spirits, and ancestors as votive offerings. Strands of prayer beads, pieces of jewelry, statues or carvings, lamps, offering vessels, painted or natural stones, shells, feathers, nuts, rose hips, berries, roots, oak galls, bones, model boats or wagons, divination sets, wands, cups, plain or decorated boxes to hold special items, small bags of magical herbs, spindles, miniature looms, knives, pieces of fur or leather: all of these and more can be dedicated to the gods, spirits, and ancestors, worn or used in their names, left on the altar or in the shrine, given away in their names or in their memory, carried and handled to remind you of them, used in ritual for them, and so on.

If the sheer number of options for devotional objects is too confusing to you, you might find it useful to do some research about what was traditional in the culture from which your gods, spirits, or ancestors came. That can help you to whittle down the range of possibilities to a more manageable list until you've had a chance to get a sense of what works best in your situation. It might also help you to have one of those "Aha!" moments that tells you what to offer.

Actions

You don't always have to offer concrete physical objects or substances to the gods, spirits, and ancestors. Actions or activities have been acceptable in many cultures, and remain a valid option today. Sports contests, for example, were held in honor of the gods in a number of traditional cultures, and excellence in athletic performance is still an entirely appropriate offering.

Many things we do in daily life can be offered up to the gods, spirits, and ancestors. Washing dishes can be turned into an offering to a hearth goddess or household spirit, or into an act of mindful gratitude dedicated to the spirits in thanks that we have hot running water to clean our homes. Work as an accountant? Dedicate your day's tasks to a deity of math and commerce, to an

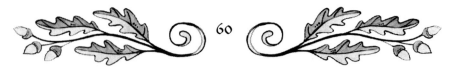

ancestor who worked as an accounting clerk, or to spirits who value order and honesty. Do you play a musical instrument or sing? Dedicate your practice sessions or your performances to a deity, spirit, or ancestor connected to music.

Actions that we engage in occasionally instead of day-to-day can also be performed as an offering. Go pick up litter in the park in honor of the nature spirits. Turn out for a volunteer work day to plant spring flowers in your neighborhood's public spaces, or to clean up a vacant lot to make a play area for local kids. Shovel an elderly neighbor's walk when it snows. Take a hot meal to a sick friend, run errands, or clean the house so your friend can stay in bed and get well. Study the languages your great-grandparents spoke, including earlier forms of English. Use your skills as a photographer or writer to document the rites and rituals you do, or your group does, in honor of the gods, spirits, and ancestors to whom the rituals are dedicated. Pitch in to help clean up fallen branches in the streets after a storm. Read up on poetic or musical forms, learn mathematical theory, improve your skills at cooking. Any of these and many more can be dedicated to the gods, spirits, or ancestors as a votive offering. So, of course, can acts of charity, which are such common acts of offering that they merit a section of their own.

Charity

Any act of charity, however large or small, can be dedicated to the gods, spirits, and ancestors; this is another ancient form of votive offering, especially where it connects to the practice of hospitality and care for the stranger or traveler. Of course many of the acts mentioned above are also acts of charity and could as well be included here. But what else can you do?

Enter a fund-raising walk in honor of one of your dead, or a deity or spirit. Make lunches for the homeless or volunteer at a soup kitchen in honor of a deity of harvest and abundance. Donate toiletries, tampons, and pads to a women's shelter as an offering to a goddess who protects abused women, or in memory of an ancestress who suffered abuse. Donate warm clothing and blankets to a homeless shelter in memory of a generous relative or one who experienced poverty, or in honor of one of the gods who made it a practice to wander the roads and visit strangers unawares. Donate money or volunteer time to a rape crisis center or a legal center that protects the rights of the poor in honor of a deity or guardian spirit who defends those who have been wronged or injured. Volunteer at a charity for veterans in honor of Uncle Joe who served in Vietnam, Granddad who was a World War II veteran, or Cousin Alice who did three turns of duty in Iraq. Pass out free coffee and cookies at a freeway rest stop as a form of hospitality to the traveler. (Several states have programs that schedule community and religious groups to take shifts at rest stops, offering snacks and beverages to travelers either for free or in return for donations.)

Whenever you perform a generous act, take a moment to stop and offer it to a god, a spirit, or an ancestor. Where possible, for example when making a donation, make it "in memory of" or "in honor of." Even if only you and your gods, spirits, and ancestors know who you're doing this to honor, the gift is still real.

Research, Meditation, and Contemplation

Your time and attention is also something you can offer, something meaningful and valuable. Take time to read up on gods, spirits, and ancestors or otherwise learn what you can about them. Research their lives, their histories, their times and places, the cultures that gave them birth and

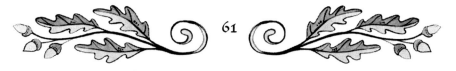

nurtured them or wrote their tales. Meditate on their stories and what you know about them. Contemplate their deeds and the meaning of their lives and actions. Consider what you can do to commemorate their virtues, to model your life on the positive aspects of their lives, to live your own life in ways that will honor their contributions. Consider their vices as well, and the negative aspects of their lives, and how you can learn from them and not repeat their mistakes. Try also to see them as whole beings, in the context of their own place and time, and to understand them as best you can. Consider what lessons they and their actions and their stories have to teach, and then put those lessons into practice in your own life. Do all of this in their honor. Above all, remember them and carry with you the awareness of them that these practices will give you.

Disposing of Perishable Offerings

It's generally a good idea, for the sake of courtesy, to dispose of perishable offerings with respect, and if possible in accordance with the appropriate cultural traditions. My food and drink offerings (other than water) are usually made in the kitchen, at the table, or out in my back garden, and I dispose of them from those locations, but the same general principles apply to tending food and drink offerings made at shrines or on altars. As a general rule, given concerns of both courtesy and hospitality, I leave food and drink only as long as it remains fresh and appetizing. You wouldn't give a friend a stale dry sandwich or a tepid glass of milk that had been sitting out in your kitchen; why offer those to the gods, spirits, and ancestors? I tend to dispose of these offerings about half an hour to an hour after making them, to allow ample time for the offerings to be consumed while still cleaning them up before they get stale. With an offering that I am going to consume myself (I rarely do this but some of my deities prefer it), I usually consume it about half an hour after offering it.

With offerings that are going to be disposed of, I compost anything that can be composted, place certain types of offerings out for animals to eat, and put the rest in the garbage. They can also be buried if you have a bit of land you can use for this purpose. I pour liquid offerings such as teas or broths onto the garden or the compost heap if suitable, or otherwise flush them down the toilet or pour them directly down the drain. Salt goes down the toilet. I pour water from my altar down the drain or on my garden, depending on circumstances. Offerings of fresh flowers or sweet herbs I leave until they have lost their scent, which usually takes a few days, or until they begin to wilt; once that occurs I compost them and wash the dish.

Devotional Practices and Travel

Travel presents a unique set of challenges to devotional practice, but with a little ingenuity, a little advance planning, and a little experience it's quite possible to work around many of them. The key is to take into account any restrictions you'll have to deal with both in the place you'll be staying and in your method of travel. Never trust to your luck to get away with something that's restricted or banned; you never know when you might get caught, or how much trouble you could land in. Instead, be willing to be honest and play by the rules.

How You're Going

Traveling by car is the least restrictive method, unless you're carpooling, have a very small vehicle or a lot of baggage, or otherwise have to cope with a lack of space. In general, you can take anything in a car that you have the room to pack. The exception is if you're crossing a state or national

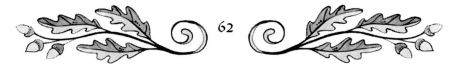

boundary into an area that restricts what items can come with you. For example, if you're going from the United States to Canada, you may not be able to take ritual items made with fur, bone, feathers, or other animal parts along with you, depending on customs regulations. Equally, going from Oregon to California, you can't bring certain kinds of fresh fruit with you because of concerns over insect pests that may have hitched a ride in or on said fruit. Research before you go to see what issues you may need to plan around. If there are restrictions in place at a border you'll need to cross, expect your vehicle to be stopped and searched, and pack accordingly.

Airline travel is the most restrictive method. You'll need to review TSA regulations before you go, and of course you'll also need to keep in mind that TSA agents are given a certain amount of leeway in deciding what to let through and what to confiscate. Items that are legal to carry or pack may be confiscated anyway, depending on the agent. You also need to take into account items that can be banned or restricted by individual airlines for whatever reasons: matches and lighters, for instance, may be barred from checked baggage but allowed in carry-on bags or purses. Research the policies of your airline as well as the TSA when deciding what to pack for checked baggage, what to pack for carry-on bags, and what to leave behind.

Train and bus travel are in the middle, in terms of restrictions; you can take more items on board a bus or train than you can take on a plane, but not as many as you can take in a car. The banned items may not always be obvious, though; Amtrak, for instance, bans jewelry in checked baggage and bans "artwork" (undefined) from any baggage, checked or carry-on. Before planning what to pack you'll also need to check the baggage options available at your starting and ending points, because some Amtrak stops don't offer checked baggage options; if you're traveling to or from one of these, you'll need to limit yourself to what can be packed in carry-on bags. Research before you go will pay off. As with airline travel, assume that your bags will be searched and pack accordingly.

It's a good idea to keep in mind that technically, federal laws about what you can and can't take on board a plane apply to buses and trains as well. Even though the TSA doesn't screen bus or train passengers in most cases, some bus lines screen passengers before boarding, and Amtrak reserves the right to screen passengers also. Due to the breadth of federal regulations, something as basic as a pocket knife is illegal to carry on all forms of public transport, including city buses. Watch what you plan to pack in your carry-on bags, purses, or laptop bags if you take the train or a bus for your journey.

Where You're Staying

As with methods of travel, some places to stay will offer you few or no restrictions, and others will have lots of restrictions. These need to be taken into account when you plan for travel.

If you're staying with understanding friends or family who have no restrictive medical conditions, you may be able to take along whatever you can bring on your chosen method of transport. Making simple arrangements in advance, such as asking the loan of a folding TV tray for your room, can cover whatever bases you need covered. If your hosts have limitations, for example asthma or allergies, or if they're not sympathetic to your religious beliefs and practices, do your best to find out in advance and plan around these limits as you would to stay in a hotel.

Hotels almost always involve significant restrictions on what you can use in your devotional practices. Most hotels ban the use of any form of flame or combustion, which includes candles, oil lamps, charcoal tablets, and fire bowls. Many also ban smoking in any form, at least in some rooms,

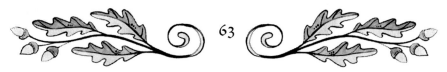

and include the use of incense, smudge sticks, or any other smoke-producing item under that ban. Some hotels ban incense and such on the double cause of smoke and combustion. If you'll be staying in a hotel while traveling, check their policies before you pack. If you're sharing a room with friends, make sure you check on their needs and limits also; be a good roommate.

Hotels also pose the practical problem of what you can do in the way of devotional practice that will neither be disrupted by the chambermaids nor cause the chambermaids to panic. Should you be going to a large established pagan gathering such as Pantheacon, the chambermaids will mostly be used to dealing with altars and shrines, and will probably leave well enough alone so long as they don't spot any violations of hotel policies or anything they think is likely to cause a problem. A hotel less familiar with alternative religious practices may have staff that are easier to upset, though, so take that into account and consider using a collection of devotional objects that will pass for a decorative arrangement.

Hostels, campgrounds, and other less structured options offer a middle ground between the comfort of a friendly private space and a rule-bound hotel. Some hostels will allow smoking or incense in the rooms; many campgrounds have established hearths or pits where fires are permitted, which would give you a place to build an offering fire. If you're going to a pagan camping event and staying in a cabin, you'll want to consider not only the campground rules and event rules but also how much space you'll have available: you may only have a bunk bed. You'll also be sharing the cabin with total strangers, who may have needs or limitations of their own, such as allergies or asthma, that you'll need to work around. However, there may be public altars on which you can make offerings, or other spaces where people can set up individual altars or shrines. If you can take a tent along and camp, of course, that gives you more leeway. Again, check the rules of the place, and what facilities are on offer, before you pack.

What to Take, How to Pack

Many of the alternative items described in the offerings section are designed with travel in mind. Going someplace where you can't have candles or incense, or using a method of travel that bans matches and lighters? Pack battery-powered tea lights or votive candles, and bring a small bag of sweet herbs. Going through the TSA screening and don't want your sweet herbs to be mistaken for a less legal variety of dried leaves? Pack some rose petals and lavender buds into a little muslin bag so it will look like a sachet, and tuck it into your checked bag. Concerned that your statue of Pan or Isis will shock the chambermaid? Make a strand of prayer beads and take that instead, or bring a token that reminds you of Pan or Isis to use in the statue's place. Worried about carrying your ritual dagger on board the train? Pack it in a sheath and put it in your checked bag.

You can always default to a small, portable collection of objects that will look like a decorative display. My traveling altar setup consists of a miniature ceramic bowl, a small square of silk, and several tiny but meaningful objects including a coin, some pebbles, and a little figurine. The whole thing fits into a zippered coin purse, and I tuck it into a packing cube among my clothing. When I get to my hotel room, I cleanse the space, wash down the surface where my altar will be, and unpack the altar bag. I use the piece of silk for an altar cloth, fill the bowl with clean water from the tap, and lay out my collection of objects to create the altar. I make daily offerings of prayer and fresh water as my basic travel devotions, and go beyond that with food, sweet herbs, or other small offerings when circumstances permit. If I'm staying with a friend or family, or attending an event with fewer

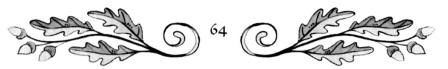

restrictions than a hotel usually has, I have another tiny ceramic dish to hold sweet herbs, a small incense burner, some miniature sticks of incense, and several other travel-sized items that I can take.

If I'm going to a place where I can't have even a makeshift altar, I carry prayer beads and other small tokens that look normal to the TSA and to hotel staff. In fact, I usually carry these types of things on any trip, even if I can take my travel altar plus all of its extra equipment, because they make it that little bit easier to focus my attention and offer prayers and meditations any time I choose. Waits in train stations and airports are easier if I've got prayer beads around my wrist or a votive token in my pocket. Many Pagan and New Age shops carry small items such as metal pocket tokens with the image of a deity embossed on them, miniature carved stone figurines of totem birds and animals, pebbles with runes or Ogham engraved on them, and so on. These make wonderful portable votive objects, don't break any rules, and aren't valuable enough to attract the interest of thieves who may have a chance to rummage through my bags.

Along with choosing what to pack in order to stay within the rules and regulations of your chosen method of travel and place to stay, you need to take into account the risk of damage or destruction for items you bring along. The double strategy of selecting items that are less likely to be damaged in the first place, and carefully packing items that are at risk, will help here. With airline travel you face a real risk of damage to items in checked baggage, and possibly also to items in overhead bins. Train and bus travel have a lower but still noticeable risk of the same. Car travel probably has the lowest risk, if the car is carefully loaded and bags with fragile items securely placed, but sudden stops or swerves can cause peril to anything that may shift unexpectedly. Furthermore, if a piece of luggage falls from the trunk or tailgate or is dropped, items inside it can still be damaged.

Although accidents will always happen, some degree of damage prevention is fairly easy to achieve if you think ahead and take precautions. While you're planning, ask yourself what the risks are with any given item. That pint of whiskey for ancestor offerings may get smashed and soak all of your clothing, your eleven-inch tapers may get snapped in half, or your favorite water bowl may arrive in two or three pieces. To some extent you can reduce these risks with careful packing: a hip flask will break less easily than a glass bottle; stiff cardboard bent and taped into a makeshift box and padded with a couple of spare socks can protect tall candles; and when it comes to pottery items, bubble wrap is your friend.

You can also take alternate items that are less likely to get damaged, though, or make some purchases when you get to your destination. Use search engines to locate the liquor store nearest your hotel so you can stock up when you arrive, bring votive candles or tea lights instead of tapers, and pack a bronze bowl in your suitcase to use for water offerings. Instead of ceramic votive statues, take along pictures. If you usually take along a framed picture, consider removing the pane of glass from the frame. Should you have creative talents with a needle, hem a placemat-sized piece of suitable fabric and embroider, needlepoint, petit point, or cross-stitch it with images and symbols of your gods, spirits, and ancestors. When you arrive, lay it out on a suitable surface and voila! Instant shrine. Consider your options, and enjoy planning something creative and fun that will fit both your needs and the restrictions you have to work within.

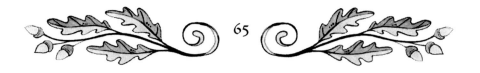

Conclusion

If you're interested in getting involved with devotional practices, you don't have to do all of the things suggested in this article, nor do you have to begin with a wide selection of them; you can pick one or two to start with, and expand from that simple beginning if you feel the need. I suggest that a good minimum would be to establish at least one altar or shrine, and make simple offerings of water, fire, incense, or sweet herbs, and prayer every day for a month. That will give you a chance to get your feet under you, do some research, listen to your intuition, and use divination or other methods of communication to help you choose where to go from there. Good luck, and have fun!

Crane Bags and the Druid Revival: A Personal Journey

Lexie Devine

Lexie Devine is currently the Grand Herald of the AODA and has an eclectic spiritual upbringing, having reached Druidry by way of Christianity, Wicca, and the Bahai faith. It has always been the nature aspect that particularly drew her to Druidry, and she feels that she has finally found her ideal spiritual home here.

While my main intention here is to tell you a personal story regarding my own experiences with crane bags and how I ended up with three of them, I'd also like to consider in this article the history of the crane bag within the Druid Revival, and the practical side of using a crane bag—size, materials, uses, and so on. In this way, maybe you will be inspired to experiment with creating your own crane bag as a working tool within your personal Druid practice.

A Little History Lesson

Before I tell you my story, here is a little bit of background about the crane bag and the Druid Revival . . . the fact is, there is no background. Strange as it may seem, the Druid Revival has no connection with crane bags, as far as we can tell. The crane bag itself originates from Irish legend. One version of the story says that Manannán Mac Lir made a bag from the body of an enchanted crane. The crane was originally a lady by the name of Aoife, a princess of the Tuatha Dé Danaan. The tale goes that she was Manannán's lover and was transformed into a crane and forced to live like this by a jealous rival named Luachra. Manannán took the transformed Aoife into his household, where she lived as a crane until her death 200 years later. When she died, Manannán made a bag from her skin and used it to hold his most precious possessions. It is also said that from time to time, great Irish leaders have been granted possession of the crane bag, and that it contains powerful objects which, though invisible to most, can be seen and used under the right circumstances by the holder of the bag.

But how did the crane bag go from the legendary bag of Manannán to an item commonly used in the Druid Revival? Well, as far as I can tell, having consulted with our Grand Archdruid and also having searched my books and online, there is a practical reason for the inclusion of a crane bag in our Druid life. It makes a great deal of sense to me to have a specific bag for ritual. It is such a useful tool, especially if you like to wander into the countryside to commune with nature, and you need to take certain items with you. The contents vary, of course, but essentially it has an inherently practical aspect, as well as a spiritual one.

If you recall the 1970s and 1980s in America, a lot of attention was being paid to the Native American shamans and their ritual tools. It was noted that they had medicine bags, which were said to hold personally selected magical items for their use. This information was absorbed by members

of the Druid community, and I am guessing the thought process went something like this.

"Druids are sort of Celtic shamans, so we need our own version of medicine bags. What can we call them, though, as we don't want to be seen as disrespectful to the Native American community?"

"What about that legend about Manannán and the crane bag? That was a magic bag, filled with important magical items."

"Perfect! We will call our bags crane bags."

Consequently, the idea of the crane bag was introduced to the AODA by one of the members, and the idea took hold. Such borrowings are a not uncommon aspect of eclectic belief systems, and once embedded can become most useful and spiritual within a personal spiritual practice.

My Three Crane Bags

One of the things I noticed very early on in my Druid Path was the importance in Druidry of the number three. It was one of those little points of interest that made me realize that Druidry was the right spiritual fit for me. You see, throughout my life the number three and multiples of it have had a significant part to play. Even my date of birth—3.11.1963—when written like this consists of a three, followed by 3 ones, and then nine, six, and three to complete the sequence. So, it came as no surprise to me when I ended up with not one, but three crane bags.

When I was first thinking about having a crane bag I thought I would make one out of cross-stitch material (known as aida in the UK), and design lots of little cross-stitch patterns that have significance to me to dot around it, then I'd line it, and have a couple of holes in the back so I could thread it onto my rope belt. Unfortunately, I might cross-stitch well, but my sewing is a disaster, so I had to shelve that plan.

Plan B was to find a suitable bag, and decorate it with beads and whatever else seemed appropriate.

Then my eldest came back from her European tour, and plan B was scratched in favor of plan C. This was because I saw what Bryony, my daughter, brought back with her.

One of the last places she had visited was Valencia, and it was there that she picked up a selection of hand-tooled leather purses of various sizes as gifts, plus a very beautiful handbag for herself. When she came home she handed out the presents, and I was stunned to be given a purse.

I became very excited because, lo and behold, a crane was etched on the purse. Manannán being my patron god, I was pretty sure he must have been looking over Bryony's shoulder when she was buying the various purses. A crane bag with an actual crane on it! Perfect! Then Bryony said to open the purse, so I did, and inside the purse was a smaller purse, also with a crane on it.

Being even more delighted when I realized I was looking at another crane, I very naturally said, "And where is crane number three?" I looked around the room, and then realized I could see the third crane. It was on the handbag Bryony had bought for herself.

Gutted! I was instantly in love with the whole collection, but Bryony was very attached to her bag, and even offering to buy it from her wasn't going to work. Then I heard myself say, "If I quit smoking, can I have it?" Well, Bryony must have thought she was onto a pretty safe bet, given the hundred or so times I had tried to stop smoking and failed, so we agreed that if I stopped smoking for three months, I could have the bag, but if I smoked a single cigarette after that, I'd have to give it back to her.

It must have been quite a shock to my dear sweet daughter that not only did I quit smoking, I did

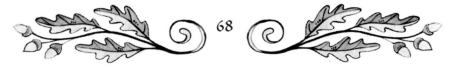

so on her birthday. So by April 13, 2006, the bag was mine, and to be fair to Bryony, she was so pleased I succeeded that she handed the bag over without a murmur. However, a few months later, in spite of the bet being fair and all, I saw her staring longingly at the bag and I offered it back to her. And she took it. But a year or so later, she handed it back to me, saying that she rarely used it, and she knew I not only loved it but had earned it, and by this time I'd been a nonsmoker for two years. Since then it has stayed with me. I have all three cranes as my crane bag, and I have not smoked since.

My three crane bags.

Your Own Crane Bag

If you don't already have a crane bag of your own but would like one, how do you go about getting one? Well, first, you need to think about what you would like to carry with you, which will help in determining the size of the bag you will want. You will also want to think about whether you want a bag that you can attach to your cord belt, or whether a bag with a shoulder strap would be preferable.

If you are the kind of Druid that likes to pack a lunch and wander into the wilderness to commune with nature as part of your ritual practices, you will likely need a good-sized bag to pack everything you will need for the day, so a large bag with inner pockets would most likely suit you

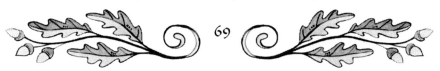

best. However, if you tend to keep your ritual work closer to home, a small bag that can attach to your belt may well suffice. Something big enough to carry a few ritual essentials but that won't be cumbersome and swing about as you work in your circle. Of course, you can always pack the small ritual bag into your bigger bag should you be the type who varies their practices according to opportunities that may arise during the day ahead.

Once the size of your bag is decided, the next step is to make or to buy. This will depend on whether you feel you have the skills to make your own bag, or whether you would prefer to buy a bag that would work well for you. Can you sew? Tool leather? Crochet? There are so many different materials to make bags from, so you may well have a skill that would work well in the design and creation of your own unique crane bag. If you prefer to go down the purchasing route—and there is nothing wrong with this option—may I suggest that you check places like charity shops (thrift shops), and second-hand stores, because you may well find the perfect bag to recycle as your crane bag, and save one from going to the landfill.

As for the contents of crane bags, that will vary enormously from Druid to Druid, depending on your personal beliefs. As an example, my three bags have different functions, so the contents naturally vary quite a bit. In my smallest one, which goes everywhere with me, I carry (among other things) a pocket prayer bead string set given to me by a friend that includes the four Druid colors from the four directions and talismans that represent Manannán and Athena, my patron god and goddess; a small stone I connect with the AODA; a four-leaf clover I found on the ground near my home a while ago; and a piece of stone from Wounded Knee—the massacre burial site in Pine Ridge, South Dakota. I was given three small stones from there and three from Pine Ridge by a lovely lady who visited her adopted Lakota family there a few years ago. She was very appreciative of all the assistance I gave to her adopted family and their friends by helping to crochet blankets for the residents of the reservation. It was her way of saying thank you to me. Those tiny little stones are more precious to me than diamonds. The middle-sized bag currently holds a compass for setting out the four directions in case I get hopelessly confused about that while out and about, a really tiny purse to hold sage or whatever I wish to take as a potential offering, a protection amulet, and a seagull feather (to represent both Manannán and Athena). It would also hold any specific jewelry I was taking with me. My particular favorite is a piece of Mohawk jewelry depicting a thunderbird. That was given to me by the same friend (her husband is a French Canadian Mohawk). The large bag is currently empty because I pack it when I know where I'm going and what I need to take with me. Items that tend to find their way in there would include candles, a South American wooden flute from Equador (Quito to be exact—another goodie given to me by Bryony), something to sit on, and my prayer shawl.

For other ideas as to what you may like to make your bag out of, and what you may like to carry in it, may I suggest you read "The Crane Bag" on the AODA website, written by John Gilbert[4].

May your bag give you years of pleasure and assistance as you go about your Druid life.

---

[4] http://aoda.org/Articles/The_Crane_Bag.html

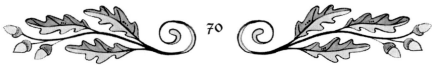

Working Through Animals: Intuitive Bone Divination
Daniel Cureton

Daniel is a Druid living and practicing in Salt Lake City, UT. He runs the Salt Lake Pagan Society, a group that seeks to provide hands-on experience in Paganism. Currently a library science master's student, he holds a BA in gender studies from the University of Utah and follows a spiritual path of Druidry, Wicca, and Santeria, all centered on the Living Earth. He is one of few people, if not the only person living, whose patron goddess is the Gorgon Medusa. In his spare time he enjoys reading, astrology, bee-keeping, tarot, and performing on his violin.

Intuitive divination focuses on the diviner, his or her relation to the divination system, and the interpretation of the shapes, signs, symbols, and messages of that system. The use of animal bones in divination dates back over 3,500 years. This article discusses ways that AODA Druids can learn to use animal bones for intuitive divination as part of the first-degree curriculum.

Bones have ancient and contemporary associations with the dead, animals, and ancestors. Ancestral worship in ancient cultures has continued into modern time, with the earliest documented rites originating in China in the Shang Dynasty around 1700 BCE (Lo, 2003, p. 36). During this period of developing ancestral rites (Gouqing, 2004-2005, p 53-54), the diviners sought answers through the use of oracle bones. The bones were written on, thrown into a fire, and the cracks and lines in the bones were interpreted afterward. The most commonly used types of bones were bovid, including cattle and water buffalo, although occasionally deer and other animals were used (Keightly, 1985, p. 6).

The use of animals in other forms for religious purposes was seen widely in ancient Egypt, with the votive mummification of cats, birds, and reptiles, numbering in the millions (Buckley, Clark, & Evershed, 2004, p. 294). Considering that the use of animals for divination and spirituality has a long history dating back over 3,000 years in different regions of the world, it's surprising that the art of bone casting isn't as popular as other forms of divination in contemporary Western culture. This in part is due to perceptions of the use of bones as "eccentric", or outside social "norms", and acceptable only around Halloween, in keeping with the widespread commercialism and promotion of that holiday.

Through practice, working bones in divination helps to develop deeper intuitive skills, meditation, awareness, and control of intuitive abilities. This is done by feeling the energies during divining sessions and traveling into the meditative spheres when working with the bones. The development of these abilities benefits the Druid in other areas of practice by familiarizing the Druid with techniques and experiences that will be similarly used in the Moon Path meditations and the Sun Path rituals in the first-degree curriculum.

Though less common than other forms of divination, contemporary bone divination is practiced in a variety of ways. A number of books speak to the practice of bone divination, not just in China but also in Greece and Africa. *Oracle Bones Divination: The Greek I Ching,* by Kostas Dervenis covers the history and style of bone casting in ancient Greece. *Throwing the Bones: How to Foretell the Future with Bones, Shells and Nuts,* by Catherine Yronwode, guides the reader to different ways of using bones in the South African Sangoma practice. And still others can be found centering on African and

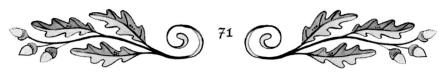

Santerian systems, such as *The Secrets of Afro-Cuban Divination: How to Cast the Dilogún, the Oracle of the Orishas,* by Ócha'ni Lele, and *The Book of African Divination Interpreting the Forces of Destiny with Techniques from the Venda, Zulu, and Yoruba.* by Raymond Buckland.

You can choose any amount of bones for reading. Depending on cultural practice (such as the Yoruba system) there may be a set number. It's generally a good measure to use as many as will fit comfortably in the hand. Depending on the type and size of the bones used and the diviner's hand, this can be as few as ten or as many as forty. Some readers will go with more or less because of magical systems, culture, or associations of numbers such as thirteen for the Goddess or twenty-one for Ellegua. Mixing bones from different animals also is possible. Please check local, state, federal, and international laws to ensure the legality of possessing the bones with which you wish to work if you plan on using more exotic types.

The following paragraphs discuss the topics of choosing to work with the bones, being energetically centered, and practicing the art of bone casting as a series of steps. These steps can be used as part of the Ovate, Bard, or Druid exploration portion of the curriculum.

The first step in working with bones or any form of divination is to identify your interest. All forms of divination are intuitive to some degree. Are you interested working with your own intuition? How about working with your inner self or other people? *The New Encyclopedia of the Occult* defines divination as "the receptive side of occult practice" (Greer, 2003, p. 134). Divination taps into the inner self, the currents of the subconscious psyche that are hidden in the day-to-day lives of most people, and pulls them to the front of the conscious mind to be examined.

The second step is to consider what form of divination appeals to you most. Literally numbering in the thousands, the most common form is tarot and oracle cards, followed by runes and Ogham. The more infrequently practiced arts include palm reading, playing cards, tea leaves and coffee grounds, wax drippings, teeth, corn, stone, coral, and shell throwing.

The third step is to find and release any unrest, negativity, biases, and emotions about bones and using animal parts in general. Some Druids find that bones do not appeal to them. Depending on background, philosophy, and life experience, the use of animal parts may or may not be the most comfortable practice. Coming to a more objective standpoint allows the mind to be open to what the bones have to teach. Releasing these energies is a recommended practice prior to doing any sort of divining so that the messages, signs, shapes, and symbols may come through clearly when throwing the bones instead of being warped and blocked by chaotic or biased emotions. Take a few controlled deep breaths. As you exhale visualize the negative currents leaving your body as dark clouds or whispers. See it leave the space you are in, leaving you only with the good energies of white or blue healing light.

The fourth step is to connect with the spirit of the animal whose bones you will be using. A simple meditation, guided spirit journey, or a trip to the natural habitat of the animals whose bones you will be using is best. Ask permission and honor the spirit of the animal so that it knows your intent. Often the animals come through with a strong presence and are willing to be totem guides as you explore working with their energy and life force, which is in the bones. If, during the meditation, the feeling is negative and permission is not given, simply set those bones aside, give thanks for the opportunity, and try a different animal. Most often those with animal guides prior to the meditation will find themselves ending up with a set of bones of their specific animal guides!

The fifth and final step is practice, practice, and more practice. The intuitive form of divination as

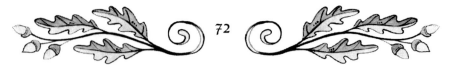

a skill is built up through practicing divining over periods of months and years, on yourself and others. The reason that this is so important to intuitive divination is that it builds the thread of patterns that come through by seeing the infinite combinations of the bones and feeling the energy each time they are cast in a different situation and context. One day they may seem to be speaking in Kanji, then the next day form the shape of a car and the word "yes" to the question, "Is purchasing a new car something I can afford right now?" This practice also builds a working knowledge of shapes, symbols, signs, and what they mean to you, the diviner.

The Bones

The real key to intuitive reading comes from being the open vessel. There is only so much information that can be gleaned from the bones, as the number will be set and there are a limited number of shapes a cast can produce. The deeper part comes from the messages being received from the animal spirit, the universe, the Living Earth, guides, yourself, and the other person if you are reading for others. Having a conversation with the person allows an opening to be formed and a bridge to be constructed on which energy and impressions can flow back and forth. This flow gets you acquainted with energy movement, if you aren't already . This is where the act of magic starts to happen, since magic is the movement of energy.

It may be helpful when first practicing to ask others to tell you their questions so that you have a platform on which to examine the shapes and understand the impressions. This helps to confirm, change, and sharpen your intuitive skills before you've gained experience. Over time, you will find that you will not need to know what the seeker asks but can feel that through the bones and intuition.

When first casting, spread the bones gently on a cloth, animal skin, or other non-slick flat surface. If candles, incense, and music help to train your mind for spirit and intuitive work, utilize those tools. Consider the external environment, outside or inside, which will be best for you to focus when casting. Environments with heavy foot traffic and noise tend to distract the mind from concentration.

After the initial cast, some find it easier to unfocus their eyes and relax the mind so that they can "listen in" on the astral chatter that can be swirling in the nethers and feel their own intuition. That thirty-second or minute-long period of silence after an initial cast could be an awkward silence to some, but is a necessary period that allows the mind and intuition to start processing what it picks

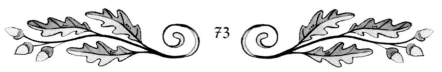

up. Don't feel pressured to fill the void with unnecessary noise and chatter, as this can interrupt the intuitive skills at work. Sometimes the messages and interpretations of the bones can be seen right away, but often it takes a little bit of examining for them to come through.

At first the bones may appear to be randomly forming images and you may not know how they apply to anything in the waking world. Don't be dismayed if at first throw the bones don't appear to be speaking—they are. This is why in the beginning, knowing the questions will help bring in and sharpen the interpretation of the meanings from the bones. The interpretations can vary widely as well. For some, the image of a horse may mean horse shamanic medicine, speed, travel, or power. To others it's about farms and support. Likewise, a house can mean support and safety, or the place of work if someone has a home business.

It is advisable to keep a journal of your readings. Write down, draw, or take pictures of the shapes and symbols that come through when first examining them so that you can go back later and reflect on what they mean and assign possible interpretations. You will already be writing as part of the Sun Path in the first degree, and journaling helps keep track of all your experiences, which is necessary for deeper reflection and understanding of Druid principals.

Part of the understanding that can be deepened when working with the animal bones is to know about the animals whose bones you've been blessed to work with. The Earth Path in the first-degree curriculum requires reading nine books about the natural world and bioregion in which you live. Some animals that exist in one bioregion do not in another. You can build on the connection with an animal's spirit by reading and studying its life cycle and habitat, engaging in conservation, adopting it as a pet, farming, or some other form of working around or with the living counterpart of the animal. Understanding the animal and where it fits into the ecosystem helps to broaden our worldview and perspective of our own place in the natural world. John Michael Greer explains this in *Mystery Teachings from the Living Earth: An Introduction to Spiritual Ecology,* showing us how tightly connected we are to the natural world:

We have, after all, the forward-looking eyes and nimble hands of the first primates that evolved to deal with the challenges of living in the dense forest of the Eocene epoch 50 million years ago. We have the hair that the earliest mammals evolved from scales to deal with the harsh winters of the Permian period 250 million years ago. The basic plan of our bodies, with four five-toed limbs extending in pairs from a central trunk, can be traced back to the first archaic lungfish that crawled ashore from the warm seas of the Devonian period 400 million years ago. Even the chemical composition of our blood mirrors that of the oceans of the Archean era more than 600 million years ago…(2012, p. 78-79).

The bones are speaking. It is up to each of us who are contemplating our place as Druids to consider listening to them and receiving their wisdom for the future as we continue on our paths. The techniques discussed above will help any person develop better intuitive skills that can be the foundation for other forms of divination and spiritual work.

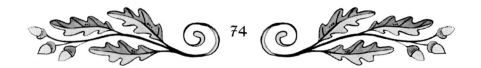

References

Buckley, S. A., Clark, K. A., & Evershed, R. P. (2004). Complex organic chemical balms of Pharaonic animal mummies. *Nature, 431*(7006), 294-299.

Gouqing, M. (2004-2005). The ancestors' drawing power. *Chinese Sociology and Anthropology 37*(2-3), 53-73.

Greer, J. M. (2003). *The new encyclopedia of the occult.* St. Paul, MN: Llewellyn.

Greer, J M. (2012). *Mystery teachings from the living earth: An introduction to spiritual ecology.* San Francisco: Weiser

Keightly, D. (1985). *Sources of Shang history: The oracle bone inscriptions of Bronze Age China (campus).* Berkeley: University of California Press.

Lo, L.K. (2003). The nature of the issue of ancestral worship among Chinese Christians. *Studies in World Christianity, 9*(1), 30-42.

Blast from the Past: Letters on Tellurism, Commonly Called Animal Magnetism

"The Alpine Philosopher" (Gioacchino de Prati) [5]

Druid teachings, like many forest trees, have tangled roots, and tracing those roots can be as complex in the one case as in the other. One of the core elements of AODA's teachings—its focus on two sources of subtle energy, the solar and telluric currents, as the basis for ritual workings—is a case in point. The teachings passed on to me when I joined the order in 2003 comprised a well-developed system, which was duly published in The Druidry Handbook (Weiser, 2006) and The Druid Magic Handbook (Weiser, 2008). Attempts to chase down the origins and earlier forms for the system, though, proved to be an exercise in frustration.

Earlier this year, though, Gordon Cooper—one of AODA's archdruids and also one of its most indefatigable researchers—discovered a series of essays from 1834 and 1835 discussing the solar and telluric currents in detail. Written under a pseudonym by Gioacchino de Prati, an Italian political exile then living in England, they appeared in The Shepherd, a weekly edited by the eccentric and irrepressible Rev. J.E. Smith, which featured many of the alternative spiritual movements of that era. The Letters on Tellurism connect the theory of the two currents to Franz Anton Mesmer's system of "animal magnetism" and to esoteric philosophies and healing practices popular in Central Europe in the late eighteenth and early nineteenth centuries, and offer an unexpected glimpse at the origins of one part of the AODA tradition—a glimpse that invites further exploration.

Letter I

DEAR SHEPHERD;—The Science of Nature is but a fragment, if it does not comprehend and embrace all the forms and shapes under which that mysterious power, which is the life and the light, reveals itself to the attentive eye of the observer. I know that it is your ardent wish to concentrate within one great focus the different modes of intellectual perception; and it is merely the universality to which you aim, that gives me the opportunity of presenting some ideas upon a subject, which at first sight must startle a great many of our contemporaries, who, immured as it were in the catacomb of partial systems, think every thing a folly which does not agree with the assumed infallibility of their puny notions.

However, in order to be perfectly understood, I shall present, under the shape of axioms, some general propositions, the truth of which must be evident to every one who is desirous to lend his attention to the philosophy of Nature.

1. All objects in the universe are living and organic. They appear in the movement of time, and in the formation of space.

2. Time and space are neither the attributes of the objects, nor mere mentalities; but necessary relations between the body and the mind.

3. Because objects are existing, they must exist at some time, and must occupy some space. The

---

[5] Transcribed by: Roana Aldinoch, Angelique Bolling, Karen Fisher, Gray Halliburton, Daniel Judy, Nancy Mezick, Kailin Miller, Ron Slabaugh, Kelly Trumble, and Bryan Wildman. Introduction by John Michael Greer.

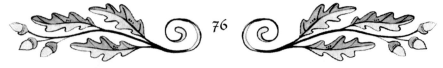

existence in time is comprehended by the mind, as the relation of succession; the co-existence in space gives to the mind the relation of co-existence. What exists in time can be calculated by the higher mathematics, under the form of fluxion. The relation of coexistence gives birth to geometry, trigonometry.

4. All objects which appear in time and space may be considered, in relation to the universe, as integral organic parts of Nature; considered singly, they must be considered as living organic beings, endowed with greater or less independence.

5. Consequently, all objects of Nature have a twofold relation; first, to the whole of which they are part—secondly, to themselves as individuals. The relation of individuals to themselves is manifested by the law of self-preservation.

6. When the living beings (objects) come in contact, there arises, according to the law of individual self-preservation, a living action and reaction—each of the two wishing to preserve itself, endeavours to destroy or overpower the other. When this occurs, the only possible results are either assimilation of one thinking with the other—that is, the formation of a new organic being, (as, for instance, water is formed by oxygen and hydrogen,) or there arises a new process of life, in which the two organic beings stand to each other in relation of polarity; the most powerful assuming the form of positive $= +$, the other the form of negative$= -$.

7. But, since nothing in the world stands insulated, or by itself, but is always in relation to other beings, consequently in continual action and reaction, the polar relations are to be found both in the largest and smallest circles of life; so much so, that polarity may be regarded as the fundamental law of the universe. Hence arises the phenomenon of general and particular sympathies.

8. If we pay attention to the planetary system, we shall find the sun action as the positive pole, $= +$, forcing the planets to form the movements around its centre; the planetary life, on the contrary, appears as the negative pole, $= -$, and its result is the double movement of the planet around the Sun and around its own axis.

9. But life and rest are contradictions; every thing in time and space is moving; but the motion is not continually increasing, nor continually decreasing, but alternately increasing and decreasing. This gives to the activity of life an oscillatory form. So, for instance, the solar power is at its summit at the epoch of perihelion, and the tellurian power is predominant in aphelion. The same oscillation is evident in the rotation of the earth around its axis; the day being the expression of the solar life; the night, on the contrary, the expression of the earthly (telluric) life.

10. A similar oscillation of polar life is also constantly to be traced in all the individual objects of the earth, since being part of the whole they must be subjected to general law. If, for instance, we examine an animal or a human being in the relation of time, we see the continual oscillation of the $+$ and $-$, and progress of development and regress of development; the two organic stages of life are similar to the two organic stages of nature, summer and winter, manhood and old age. If we consider them in the relation of space, or as organic beings, the male appears as the positive, $+$, the female as the negative, $-$; yea, the sensitive system is the positive, $+$, the vegetative the negative, $-$. Even among the nerves, the muscles, the veins and the arteries, the lungs and the heart, the same relation of polarity is undeniable.

11. All objects of the earth being subjected, as parts of the whole, to the law of polarity, must be classed under a solar or telluric relation.

THE ALPINE PHILOSOPHER.

Letter II

In my former letter I have exposed the general laws of nature, which I mean to apply to the object of my researches.

1. The animal magnetism, or tellurism, is that action and reaction operated by two organic beings, in which the telluric power acts in relation to the solar power, as the positive pole.

2. The essence of the telluric action and reaction, therefore, consists in the preponderance of the quality of telluric life in the agent; though in regard to the *quantity* of the effects, the agent himself may be considered as positive; which action and reaction manifests itself in the different degrees of somnambulism, or night-life, produced in the patient.

3. Since every object on earth is an analogue (or type) of the solar or of the telluric agency, every object is likewise magnetic or anti-magnetic.

4. In the same way that the solar agency produces a certain physiological series of phenomena called watching (or waking), the telluric agency produces a certain physiological series of phenomena called sleep. The physiologists have hitherto neglected this second original form of life; being ignorant of the fundamental laws of existence, they have considered sleep as a mere absence of activity. Hence their futile attempts to explain some of the most striking phenomena, such as dreams, somnambulism, &c.

5. The natural sleep, however, is night-life, or telluric life; it is the half of the cyclus of life; and has its analogue in the change of day and night in the evolution of our planet. Sleep, as the polar antithesis of watching, is related to it like the negative pole of the magnet to its positive pole. Consequently it must present general phenomena of its own kind, exactly corresponding to the phenomena produced by watching in a polar antithesis; which phenomena are the following:

6. The influence of the solar life is diminishing at night, and that of telluric life is increasing; which is visible in the contraction of the muscles in animals, and of the contraction of fibres in plants. This contraction is increasing, and reaches its maximum at midnight, and declines towards the break of the day.

7. The activity of the sensitive system decreases: hence, when sleep is approaching, the sensitiveness for outward influences is almost entirely gone, so that all voluntary movements are at an end. On the contrary, the activity of the vegetative system is increasing; digestion, assimilation, and growth are now active. The wounds are closing faster. Even the plants grow faster at night than during the day-time.

8. In the animal system the activity of the movement of blood is augmented. Hence fevers are generally increasing ; the skin becomes warmer, redder, and more turgid.

9. In the nervous system the function of the brain is dormant, whilst the function of the ganglia is in full activity. During the day-time, and whilst man is watching, the intelligent functions overrule, as positive pole, the faculty of feeling. During the sleep, feeling and imagination overrule the intellectual faculties, and appear in their positive activity. The self-consciousness of *reason* gives way to the self-consciousness of *instinct*. The reason, whilst we are watching, gives birth to ideas and to language; the instinct, whilst we sleep, gives birth to dreams, which are the hieroglyphical language of telluric life.

10. In the ancient world, whilst intelligence had not grown to the summit of self-consciousness, the influence of telluric life was stronger—indeed the two poles were not yet so opposite. The race

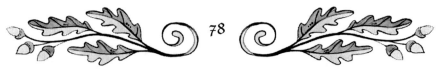

of mankind was following more the instinct, and all their philosophy, religion, and arts, were rather a produce of feeling and imagination, than of reason and self-determination.

11. This physiological view of the state of the human race explains at once all the doings of the prophets, the priests, the sibyls, the poets, the magicians, the seers, the druids, which the learned ignorance of later ages has declared as self-conscious deceptions. All these phenomena are true. They have been the produce of telluric life.

12. The dreams appear in a threefold form, simple, allegorical, and anthropomorphistical. In the first form, the instinct, freed from the shackles of reason and understanding, has a clear intuition of things that exist at a certain distance in space, or happen at a certain distance of time. In fact, time and space being only the relations of existing things, and viewed by the medium of reason, such relations are no barriers for the instinct, which stands in the medium of the telluric influence in the immediate contact with the objects themselves.

The second form represents things that are, or will happen, in a poetical form. Take, for instance, Joseph's dream in the Bible,—to explain which language a proper study is necessary, the Oneiroscopia. The third form, which is the highest, occurs when the dreamer fancies a certain angelic, demoniac, god-like being to unveil to him the present or the future. The genius of Socrates, the angels of the old prophets, the dove seen by the apostle, are examples of this third form of dreams.

THE ALPINE PHILOSOPHER.

Letter III

If all in nature is subjected to the general law of Polarity; if the most general form under which the law of polarity manifests itself on earth is the phenomenon of solar and telluric life, the whole race of mankind, as well as the single individuals, must be subjected to the same general law.

1. In fact, if we consider the history of the human race, we find it following in its development the physiological laws of solar and telluric life.

2. The solar life of mankind consists in the manifestation of intelligence and liberty; the telluric life, on the contrary, consists in the manifestation of instinct and necessity. The more mankind is subjected to the telluric life, the more will instinct and necessity govern the world, and the expression of all actions, morals, and feelings will be concentrated in one focus, called belief or faith. The more mankind is subjected to the influence of solar life, the more will intelligence and liberty govern the world. The general expression of all actions, morals, and feelings will be also concentrated in one focus, called knowledge.

3. But since polarity is the universal law, there can be in the history of mankind neither faith without knowledge, nor necessity without liberty, but both must always exist, and will ever exist together: the only difference between one epoch and the other will be their + or -, or the preponderance of the one over the other. The coexistence of the two aspects of life, the positive and the negative, and their oscillatory process was allegorically expressed under the struggle of two principles.

4. The ancient world presents the phenomena of telluric influence. It is the night of mankind; here wonders, divinations, dreams, prophesies, oracles, and revelations, follow one another. As the animal by instinct builds the most wonderful cells or nests, moves and travels from region to region,

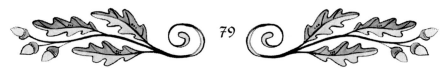

distinguishes the healing or nourishing food from that which is poisonous and unwholesome; in the same way the seers, the magicians, the priests, the poets, the artists of the old world, performed those deeds which the most enlightened among the children living under the solar life can now neither understand nor believe. Thus the waking individual can scarcely comprehend and believe that which he has dreamed or done during that part of life which he calls sleep.

5. The ancient world had reached the summit of telluric life when Christ and the Christian had made their appearance. The earth was then on the highest point of somnambulism. By the means of Christ, and through the Christian religion, the family of mankind began to awaken. Christ's wonders are as it were the morning dreams of one who is near to open his eyes to the beams of that centre of light that calls forth the solar life in nature.

6. This philosophical bird's-eye view of the past can alone explain the twofold nature of Christ, and the twofold forms under which Christianity must appear.

7. Primitive Christianity, with its wonders, with its belief, with its instinctive necessity, is the last and most luminous aspect of telluric life. Christianity, with its new world and its new heaven, with its law of love and liberty, with its appeal to reason, belongs to the solar life; hence the discovery of printing, the Copernican system, the manifold discoveries in all sciences, and the science of tellurism, or animal magnetism, could only occur under the influence of solar life.

8. Our readers must, however, bear constantly in mind that the general law of Nature being polarity, and each pole being a constituent part of the whole, the preponderance of a pole over the other does not imply the destruction or the absence of the other. During the telluric life of mankind, the solar life was also existing, but subordinate to the telluric life; and, *vice versa*, when the solar life shall have reached its summit, the telluric life will still exist, only in a subordinate state.

9. Since nations and individuals are not insulated in Nature, but stand to each other in the relation of polarity, there will be always nations and individuals who in relation to the others, will be representative of one of the two poles.

10. The Jews, in relation to the Gentiles, were the representatives of the positive pole; and the Jews were the negative pole in relation to the Egyptians. At present the whole east is, in comparison with the west, in a state of somnambulism.

11. The religious books of the Hindoos, the Zend-Avesta, the Bible, the Talmud, the Koran, are not inventions of designing priestcraft, but divine dream-books of inspired seers.

12. The gods, or the god of these religions were but allegories, or personifications of some principles of life. They were but partial, individual creations of telluric influence.

13. The diagram of the whole history of mankind, as viewed by the eyes of the philosopher, is the following:

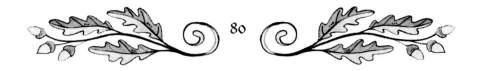

UNIVERSAL LAW

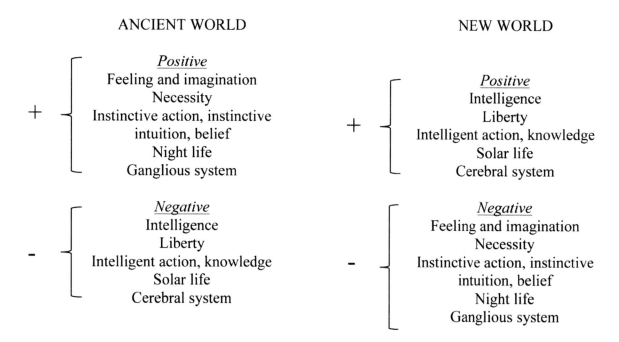

ANCIENT WORLD

+ {
Positive
Feeling and imagination
Necessity
Instinctive action, instinctive
intuition, belief
Night life
Ganglious system
}

- {
Negative
Intelligence
Liberty
Intelligent action, knowledge
Solar life
Cerebral system
}

NEW WORLD

+ {
Positive
Intelligence
Liberty
Intelligent action, knowledge
Solar life
Cerebral system
}

- {
Negative
Feeling and imagination
Necessity
Instinctive action, instinctive
intuition, belief
Night life
Ganglious system
}

Positive (+) and Negative (-) equal to the whole Nature.

THE ALPINE PHILOSOPHER.

Letter IV

It is the general custom of authors to introduce their works to the notice of the public, wrapped up in a long robe, called preface. Therein the authors are like the Egyptian high priests, who, in order to secure an everlasting duration to their mummies, after having spiced, pickled, and fumigated the bodies, wound whole pieces of linen around the royal relics. In a similar way, a friend of ours has written a book of 552 pages, of which only 446 are preface, which I was tempted to compare with the tail of a comet, the kernel of which, according to modern astronomers, is nothing but condensed gas.

But I do not mean to disparage the authors of long prefaces, nor to nullify the author of the longest one. That would be the same as if I was silly enough to criticise Nature, the law of which is infinite variety of forms and structures. I am telling a mere fact, for which I claim for myself the privilege of interrupting the dogmatical course of my letters, and to request my readers to consider them as a kind of preface. I dislike sameness; indeed, were I obliged to live in a world where all human beings were cast in one mould, either after the spiritual pattern of the Platonic school, or after the material model of ancient or modern Epicureans, methinks I might be tempted to imitate the example of some love-sick heroes of modern romance, and hang myself for mere ennui.

But happily, the world is not, and will never be, such as the *one-sided* fools fancy to make it.

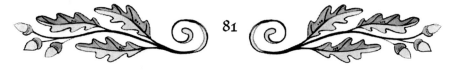

Sameness is contrary to the eternal laws of Nature, that delights in variety, and has made the bipolar principle the basis of advancement and progressiveness. Beauty, virtue, truth, happiness, all after which mankind is striving, are like unto a masterpiece of musical genius; instead of being the eternal unison of the same note, they are the variation of seven notes, of flats and sharps, of quick and slow movements and expressions,—where the soft flute and the noisy trumpet, the merry violin, the manly oboe, the time-keeping violoncello and bassoon, and all other string and wind instruments, reveal each in their kind a progressive musical composition, and form a whole of heavenly harmony. For him who has no music in his heart, these observations are lost; but I hope they will not be lost for the readers of the *Shepherd*! because how would they otherwise be able to understand the science of the Harmony of Nature?

My former letters are but the preface of the present one, and of the whole series of those in which I shall continue to converse with our readers, whom I wish to tease and puzzle, in order to call forth some observation! What? Have I not succeeded in puzzling a compositor? Why should I not succeed in puzzling any of our readers? I will try it.

The religious and historical writings of the Jews, and of all eastern nations, those of the Greek and Romans, those of the German nations, are all relating facts, which have been rejected by our contemporaries as mere inventions of designing hypocrites, or deplorable illusions of deluded believers.

Such facts are, for instance, the healing of disease by the mere manipulation of the prophets, or by the strong belief of the patient; the prophetic dreams, the prophesies, or the witchcraft. For instance, we read in the Bible of the wonderful restoration to life of a youth by the prophet, of the restoration of sight of Tobias by the angel; we are informed by the historian that the Egyptian priests brought their sick into the temples, where they fell asleep, and during the sleep the gods revealed the remedies for their diseases. The Emperor Hadrian cured blindness; and no less a man than Tacitus relates that the Emperor Vespasian healed blind and lame people by manipulation (imposition of hands).

Apollonius of Tyana performed as many and as wonderful cures as any recorded in the New Testament. The Jewish sect of the Essenes possessed also the power of healing diseases by manipulation. The dissenters of the primitive Christian church, called the Montanists, from Montanus, performed also many wonderful cures; indeed these cures were so striking, that one of the fathers of the church became an apostate, seduced by the magical cures of these dissenters.

The records of witchcraft are coeval with the history of mankind. There is no nation without prophets, and prophetic dreams; none without wonders and wonderful cures.

Now, I say in the teeth of all philosophers, that these facts are true. Witchcraft and divination, the power of healing by manipulation, and by the force of the will and of the belief, are as indisputable as the phenomena of galvanism and electricity.

Animal magnetism has discovered this hidden part of nature, and has elevated to a science that which, being hitherto practised by mere instinct, has justly deserved the name of superstition. In fact, superstition is but the negative pole of religion, and religion is but the negative pole of science.

Gentle readers, keep the bipolar law of nature steadfastly in your minds; let it be the compass that guides your ship on the voyage of discovery, and you will reach the heavenly shore of truth.

THE ALPINE PHILOSOPHER.

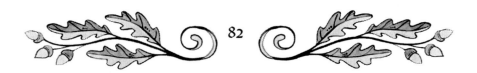

Letter V

A Traveller was returning from a long journey; his home stood like a heavenly garden before the eyes of his imagination. With every step he made his heart was beating louder and louder; for he had left for many years his native land, and his thatched cottage, with the overhanging fruit-trees, the Eden of his childhood; wherefore he doubled his steps the nearer he came to his dear home. But when he had reached the summit of the mountain, on the opposite slope of which his cottage was situated, a dark night spread a black veil over his path.

"What shall I do in this darkness!" sighed the good man. "Who will lead me safe over the mountain? Shall I lose myself in the woods, and become a prey of the hungry wolf that infests the forest?"

Whilst he stood still uttering these complaints, and looking whether he could discover any human trace, he beheld at a distance a light, a bright moving light; a God-send to the weary, forlorn wanderer; and refreshed with hope, he hastened towards the friendly element.

Whilst proceeding in the direction of the moving light a thundering voice called from a distance, "Stop, wanderer, stop! If thou proceedest farther on thou art the son of Death." He stopped and hearkened, and he heard as it were the splashing of oars, and after awhile he could distinguish a boat approaching. And the boatman called to the wanderer, and said, "Man, what seduced thee from the right path, and brought thee to the brink of death?" "It was that friendly light that shines before me," replied the wanderer.

"A friendly light!" exclaimed the fisherman, who in the meanwhile had landed; "It is a deceiving flame, the offspring of corrupted marshes!" In fact it was an ignis fatuus; or rather two or three, or more, which from time to time flame and disappear.

They had all disappeared, and the traveller returned hearty thanks to his preserver. Yet the fisherman answered and said, "Why should one man allow another to die in error, instead of showing him the right way? We must both offer our thanks to God; I, for having been chosen as his instrument to preserve thee from perdition; thou, because saved from the brink of a precipice, where a false light was alluring thy erring steps."

The fisherman, who by long habit knew to find his way in the darkness, took the wanderer under his arm and led him safe down the mountain, and placed him on the high road, which conducted him in a straight line to his native cottage. And here I will leave him, opening the well-known door, and embracing his dearly beloved ones. And I will turn myself to you, my gentle readers, for whom this parable is intended.

The false science, the science of individualism, of sectarianism, of one principle, is like unto that shining deceiving offspring of corrupted marshes. The bipolar philosophy, the science of nature, applied to all the business of life, is the friendly fisherman that brings you safely to your homes. And do you know what your homes are? Those four walls within which you eat and drink? Surely not. The towns in which you work yourselves to death to feed in luxury a few idlers? Surely not. Your home is the whole of nature, where knowledge is the fruit that refreshes and strengthens us, and makes us like unto gods.

Now this science of nature teaches us also how to subdue diseases and restore health; yea, I hope it will in future time teach us to subdue death. This science is but in its beginning, though it has been put into practice partially and instinctively in all ages. And because the people who exercised it in former ages, did not know the true reason of their working, they ascribed this power to God or to

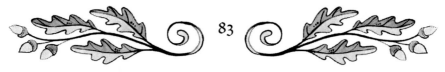

the devil, according as they supplied it with good or bad intentions.

In fact they were not entirely mistaken in ascribing this power to one of the two principles because the principle of this power of healing is *spiritual*, and diseases are also *spiritual*.

The principle of healing is the spirit of light and of life; the principle of disease is the spirit of darkness and of death. Hence he who can forgive the sins can heal the disease. The first physicians were priests. The snake, which was the symbol of the fall of man, is also the symbol of the art of healing; because, in order to cure a disease you must create a disease; and the snake and the cross are both necessary to salvation.

Since there is but one spirit, the Spirit; one life, the Life; and since health and disease are but the positive and negative of the same spirit, and of the same life, there can be but one principle of healing.

This one principle of healing is the bipolar magnetic, or solar and telluric. All other modes of treatment are but secondary means, which act chemically and mechanically, more to the injury than to the benefit of the human frame. If they act otherwise, they act magnetically; for instance, bark acts magnetically in all cases where the disease has assumed the shape of intermittence; the cow-pox acts magnetically in bringing forth a principle counteracting contagion; all epidemic diseases, the plague, the cholera morbus, the marsh fevers, are produced by solar or telluric influences, and disappear by changes in the keys of the great panharmonicon (*universal harmony*) of nature.

The magnetic origin of diseases explains the phenomenon of their being under the influence of certain numbers. Indeed the mystical importance given by the old philosophers, physicians, and divines, to certain numbers, is owing to the instinctive intuition of the magnetic solar and telluric oscillators. It is a fact that must strike every impartial observer, that in the 3d, 7th, 9th, 11th, 14th, and 28th day, fevers and other diseases, both acute and chronic, are in a state of increase or decrease.

It is a fact that none can deny, that some mental disorders, some nervous complaints, such as epileptic fits, St. Vitus's dance, and other like disorders, break forth with greater violence during the spring tides. So great is the concord and harmony of nature.

Modern physiologists, for instance, Schubert, in his Universal History of Life, Goïres in Munich, Professor Walter in Bohu, Professor Burdach in Königsberg, have found that the influence of the numbers three and seven in the development, cause changes in the human frame. It is a well-known fact, that a child may live, if born in the seventh month, and will not live if born in the eight month. Every seven years the whole body of man is changed by an organic transubstantiation. The 7th, 14th, 21th, 35th, 49th, and 56th years, generally produce changes in the human body; and the 63d year is the grand climacteric, being the multiplication of 9 by 7.

The number nine is the most remarkable of all the units. Thus when nine is multiplied by any figure or figures, the digits in the product being added together make up the number nine. Thus, for example, $9 \times 3 = 27$, and $2 + 7 = 9$; again, $9 \times 40 = 360$, and $3 + 6 = 9$.

I shall not follow up the magnetical power of numbers in the polarity of light, in the formation of colours, in the wonderful combination of sounds. I will only mention that even in that which is called inorganic nature, for instance, the elective affinities in chemistry, the formation of strata in geology, and the crystallizations, the influence of numbers is as evident as is the construction of animals and plants.

Pythagoras was the first who by an act of magnetic ecstacy had the intuition of the mystical

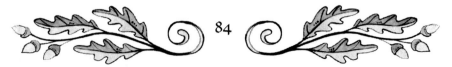

science of numbers. The means adopted by him instinctively to produce this ecstacy will be found to correspond with the means discovered by the science to bring forth that highest state of telluric, or night life, called somnambulism. I shall finish this letter, presenting my ideas upon the nature of the human soul, and its bipolar nature.

The soul is the spiritual principle of life. Life being bipolar, the human soul must also present a bipolar activity. Acting as the representative of the solar principle, it appears as reason and intelligence, and as the plastic or forming principle. The soul forms both the reasoning faculties and the *organs of thinking*. In the character of the telluric principle it appears as instinct and sense, and forms the perceptive faculties, and the *organs of sensation*. As the principle of intelligent life, it forms the brain and cerebral nerves; as the principle of instinctive life, it forms the ganglia and the sympathetic nerves.

In order to support these two extremes it forms the animal system, blood, lymph. From the different proportions of these different organs of the soul arise the difference of temperaments, capacities, and passions. The philosophers who pretended that men had three souls—the vegetative, intelligent, and animal soul—were correct in the triad; but for want of a knowledge of the science of polarity, mistook the two extremes and their middle term for three different individualities.

THE ALPINE PHILOSOPHER.

Letter VI

Alterius non sit qui suus esse potest.—Paracelsus
"Be not a copy if thou canst be an original."

In the house of my parents there was a room called the library, the walls of which were ornamental with prints, each print representing the effigies of some learned man. Here lived in peaceful harmony men of the most opposite opinions, Luther and Calvin, Hogstraten and Servetus, Dante and Pope Boniface, Cujace and Puffendorf, Machiavelli and Savonarola, Wicliff, and Cardinal Bellarmin, Galen and Van Helmont, and many others whom I scarcely can recollect. Yet, among this worthy assembly, there was a man whose countenance is constantly present to my imagination, namely, Theophrastus Bombasta Paracelsus.

The reason why this man's physiognomy made such a powerful impression upon my mind is not so much owing to the originality of his features as to the originality of the motto which is annexed to his print; which motto pleased me so much that I adopted it as my own. To this circumstance I owe my first acquaintance with the science of Nature. It is quite natural that, fond as I was of the motto of this extraordinary man, I was also interested to make a nearer acquaintance with him by reading his works, his life, his opinions. This study involved me in a series of researches of the most curious kind; and I must candidly confess that I regard Paracelsus as one of my greatest benefactors. From him I learnt to seek for knowledge in the great book of Nature; he taught me to dispose of the pretended wisdom of the schools, and to strive to become myself a master of that philosophy which does not deal with empty names and forms, but draws its nourishing milk from the everflowing, refreshing brook of life.

Paracelsus is the father of modern chemistry, and of the science of magnetism; he has shared with all men of genius the fate of being persecuted and misrepresented by his contemporaries. I

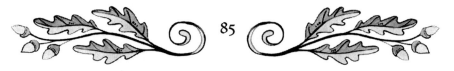

have visited his tomb in Salzburg. Over his tomb hangs his portrait, over which is the motto, which I have adopted as my own, and stands at the head of this letter.

To-day I will entertain my readers with the phenomena of magnetic or telluric treatment. I know that my statements will draw upon me the censure of being either a deceiver or a dupe; yet I stand boldly as the defender of truth; I relate not opinions, but facts; for these facts I have not only the evidence of the greatest philosophers and physicians of Germany, Sweden, Denmark, Russia, and Holland, but I have also my own experience. I have myself exercised this art for five years, and collected a great number of data, which I shall lay before the public in some future letters. Indeed, I am so convinced of the truth of these facts, that I offer myself to treat magnetically any case of disease that should be entrusted to my care. I will show to the public that all the phenomena are not only possible, but true.

The magnetical phenomena are produced by the concentration of the will, by manipulation, and by the baquet, or other solar or telluric influences of those substances, the diagram of which is annexed to this letter. Each of these means may produce the same phenomena, but the phenomena vary according to the nature of the disease; and indeed they are varying almost in every individual, both in intensity and in form.

But since all diversity in Nature has a tendency to uniformity and unity, the differences may be reduced to a kind of systematic classification. The most general result of the magnetic treatment is the cure of all diseases, even of those that have hitherto baffled the skill of medical art.

The diseases of the sensitive and reproductive systems are those which have offered the most luminous instances of the efficacy of the telluric treatment; all sorts of nervous diseases, tetanus, St. Vitus's dance, epilepsy, paralysis general and partial, tic doloreux, convulsions, blindness, deafness, lameness, all forms of scrofula, and cutaneous diseases, all sort of hemorrhoids and constipations, and fevers. All these species of diseases have disappeared under the magnetic treatment, either without any critical revolution or metastasis, or by means of critical perspirations, issues, &c. For instance, a lady, who, for seven years, had suffered mortal pains under the influence of the most violent migrane, was perfectly restored to health by means of animal magnetism, this treatment causing an erysipilas, which had been improperly cured, to reappear. A similar instance of improperly-cured cutaneous disease, that caused monthly epileptic attacks, was discovered by magnetism. After a few weeks telluric treatment under the baquet, the cutaneous disease reappeared, and the patient was cured of epilepsy; by continuing the magnetic treatment, the cutaneous disease was also subdued.

But in most instances the magnetic treatment causes other phenomena. The first degree of magnetical action shows itself by a kind of uneasiness, nausea, or yawning. The second degree shows itself to the patient by his being compelled to shut his eyes. Sometimes, after two or three days' treatment, the patient falls asleep, overpowered by the magnetic influence.

Third degree.—The sleep becomes more intense, and begins to transform itself into somnambulism. In this state the patient is opening and shutting his eyes as if in a convulsive state; he begins to be insensible for any thing around him except for the magnetiser; he begins to contract the lips as if to speak, but he is unable to do so.

Fourth degree.—The telluric life manifests itself by a deeper somnambulism; the patient begins to speak some broken words, and to direct the mode of manipulation; his first want is for magnetic water.

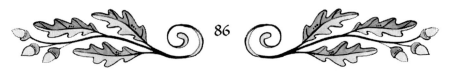

Fifth degree.—Confirmed somnambulism. The somnambulist begins, as it were, to live his second life; the strongest sympathy towards the magnetiser shows itself; the voice becomes more harmonious, the language purer; the antipathy towards other persons present shows itself also. In these stages the sensitive and perceptive faculties forsake the usual organs, and concentrate themselves in one focus, the plexus solaris. (The plexus solaris is a kind of bundle of nerves, united in a kind of globes, of the substance of the brain, placed in the cavity of the stomach). A word spoken to this part is heard by the somnambulist, though the loudest sounds have no effect upon his ear. In this stage the somnambulist begins to acquire the power of examining himself; it is the first stage of instinctive self-intuition. Many have decided with the accuracy of a dissector the internal structure of their body, and indicated the site of their disease; they have determined before-hand the whole or a part of the course of their cure, and foretold the attacks several months before to a minute.

Sixth degree.—All those phenomena announced before in a more intense degree. In this state the somnambulist is able to prescribe for himself and for others.

Seventh degree.—The last degree is that of the ecstacy or clairevoyance. This stage, though the rarest, is one of the most wonderful. The somnambulist does not only hear, but also sees and smells with the stomach. Sometimes he sees and smells with the finger-tips and with the crown of the head.

Time and space have no more limits for the perceptive faculties. They view things passing at a distance, and foretell things which have to pass in the future. The dependence under which they have been placed under the magnetiser, seems to change into a powerful action and reaction; so that often they read the magnetiser's most secret thoughts. Sometimes the two beings seem to have but one thought; in this state the somnambulists do not only predict and prescribe their cure, but also they prescribe the cure of others who live at a great distance. But how will our readers startle when I tell them that the somnambulists, in this state, have also caused distant persons to see their apparitions, and to have exercised their magic influence over distant friends, so as to advise them in visions of threatening dangers! A peculiar feature of this stage is the highly religious feeling that is evinced in them.

The spiritual life, as feeling itself free from the enchaining form to which it is bound, seems to soar higher and higher to the living source of life and of bliss, that is, the soul of souls, whose name is unknown, but whose life is creation, intelligence, and love, and whose existence is manifested in its bipolar revelation.

O that I could bring before the believers and unbelievers the somnambulists in their degree of ecstacy, and ask them where is that unfeeling, fatal goddess, which they call Nature, or where is that tormenting, evil principle, whom blind fanaticism worships as God!

O there is a God; but God is the One:

He is the life, the love, and the light.

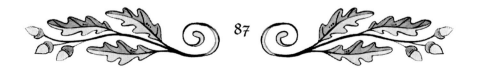

Diagram of the Positive and Negative Telluric Influences.

Positive (+).	Negative (−).
Night	Day
Darkness, heat, moonlight	Daylight
Violet ray	Red ray
Music: Flat minor	Music: Sharp Major
Magnetism, galvanism, electricity, South pole	Magnetism, galvanism, electricity, North pole
Zinc	Silver
Precious stones	Glass, silk, inflammables
Fixed metals, gold, platina	Volatile metals, kali, ammonium
Ganglious system	Cerebral system
Desiring faculties, feelings	Intellectual faculties
Imagination	Reason
Carbon	Nitrogen
Oxygen	Hydrogen
Acids.	Alkalis.

THE ALPINE PHILOSOPHER.

Letter VII

"E piu se muove!" – Galileo
"And yet it moves!"

If I should be asked whether the great discoveries in arts and sciences are owing to the superior intelligence of men, or to some peculiar revelation of God, my plain answer would be, "Most surely, the greatest discoveries owe their existence to God's revelation." Indeed, the intelligence of individuals is, in regard to the absolute divine intelligence, nothing but the organs by which and through which the great act of revelation is performed. It is therefore but a vulgar error to ascribe all discoveries to mere accident; as if, in a world in which the least atoms are, in their movements, attractions, repulsions, combinations, compositions, and decompositions, birth, growth, death, and reproduction, subjected to the eternal law of bipolarity; I say, it is as if, in a world where the spirit of God is daily, hourly, yes, at every minute, repeating the work of creation, anything could happen like chance or accident! And most surely it was not a blind chance, but a wise divine decree, which caused the discovery of animal magnetism to be revealed to a physician, at an epoch in which the generality of physicians and philosophers had been the most active instruments in spreading that system which considers matter as the only principle of life.

Frederick Anthony Mesmer, the discoverer of animal magnetism, was born on the 5th of May, 1737, at Stein, a small town of Switzerland, situated on the banks of the Rhine. In his earliest youth he evinced a great fondness for the study of nature; he told me once that, when a boy, his greatest pleasure was to retire into solitary spots, and there to amuse himself in contemplating the operations of insects, the flight of birds, and in comparing the different shapes of plants, and herbs, and

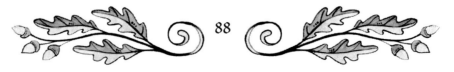

mosses. He remained often out in the fields till late in the night, when the rising of the stars and the moon filled his mind with deep sacred feelings. "I was then," said he, "under the magnetical influence of Nature; the full flood was streaming above, below and around me. My mind was full; but I did not know what was working in me."

His parents, who were respectable, though not wealthy, discovered in Anthony a great fondness for natural sicence, and used their greatest efforts to make him a physician. After completing his preparatory studies at the Swiss schools, he was sent to Vienna to study medicine. At that time the university of Vienna enjoyed a high reputation as a medical school. His professors were Van Swieten and Haen.

He studied with great application, and in the year 1766 he obtained the degree of M.D., on which occasion he began to show his lofty and independent mind. A youth, in the presence of professors, who were incarnate fact-and-experiment-mongers, in a town and in a century in which nothing but tangible theories were admitted as true, Mesmer published a pamphlet, in which he attempted to demonstrate the influence of the planets on the human body. All his acquaintances, his masters, indeed the whole tribe of fashionable professors, philosophers, and literati, were so indignant at what they called an attempt to bring back old ignorance and superstition, that they turned their backs upon him, and designated him as half diseased in his mind.

Mesmer laughed at his scoffers, and settled himself as a physician in the Austrian capital. There he began to study deeper and deeper the science of Nature; and by endeavouring to trace one universal principle of life, which could be employed as a principle of cure, he first took electricity to be this principle. Instructed by experience of the fallacy of this surmise, he turned his enquiries toward metallic magnetism; and, after having devoted his attention to it, he began to try experiments with the artificial loadstone, for which purpose he procured magnets of different forms and dimensions, which he first applied to the cure of local diseases, and afterwards to the cure of nervous affections.

His attempts succeeded; and in the year 1775 he laid his discoveries open to the world. But the world was not willing to received them. He was treated both as a fool and a dupe; which opposition, however, instead of deterring, strengthened Mesmer in his endeavours.

In the meanwhile several people of quality applied for his magnetic assistance, and several happy cures put him in the situation of forming a private hospital. Here, whilst treating some patients with the artificial loadstone, he noticed some phenomena of somnambulism. He observed more closely, and saw that these phenomena were not accidental, but dependent upon the magnetic treantments. Finally, by repeated trials, he found that the artificial magnet was quite unnecessary for the production of these phenomena; and all at once his eyes were opened, and the divine thought flashed into his mind; the universal fluid or flood was found; he named it "Animal Magnetism."

After this great discovery, Mesmer assumed the airs of a magician, and began to perform his cures under a veil of mystery, through which no one was able to penetrate. Some believed that he was working his cures by concealed loadstones; others, that he used some new hidden electrical apparatus. The alchemists swore that he had found the philosophers' stone; bigots said he had a compact with the devil; unbelievers accused him of being a cheat and impostor.

Mesmer paid little attention to these calumnies, but continued his practice with great success. This, however, excited the envy of the whole profession; and having injured the pecuniary interests of the emperor's head physician, the miracle-doctor, being a foreigner, was most graciously ordered

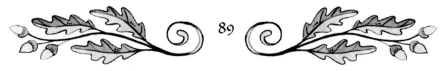

to quit Vienna within twenty-four hours, and to keep clear of the imperial dominions for ever! Indeed, such was the fury of the profession against magnetism, that a law was enacted by which physicians and surgeons were prohibited from magnetising, under the penalty of forfeiting their licence, and the profane were forbidden under a severe corporal punishment. Consequently, he left Vienna in 1777, and after vising his native land, came, in February, 1779, to Paris.

The learned men of that capital had bent their views in quite an opposite direction; instead of finding support, he was laughed at as a dreamer. But his energy being unrelenting, he at length succeeded in gaining the support of Dr. D'Eslon, a member of the faculty of Paris. Under the auspices of this physician, he published, in the year 1779, his first memoir on animal magnetism.

The science being yet in its infancy, Mesmer's theory could be no otherwise than a mixture of error and truth. It was the following:—

"There is a reciprocal influence (action and reaction) between the planets, the earth, and animated nature." (True.)

"The means of operating this action and reaction is a most fine, subtle fluid, which penetrates everything, and is capable of receiving and communicating all kinds of motions and impressions." (Fanciful.)

"This is brought about by mechanical, but, as yet, unknown laws." (False.)

"The reciprocal effects are analogous to the ebb and flow." (Beautiful analogy! the germ of the theory of polarity.)

"The properties of matter and of organisation depend on reciprocal action." (True.)

"This fluid exercises an immediate action on the nerves, with which it embodies itself, and produces in the human body phenomena similar to those of the loadstone; that is, polarity and inclination." (Here was the great mistake of Mesmer, of confounding the original law of polarity and life, with the effect of a particular fluid.)

"Hence the name of animal magnetism." (A wrong name.)

"This fluid flows with the greatest quickness from body to body, acts at a distance, and is reflected by the mirror like light; and it is strengthened and propagated by sound." (The truth of these facts is undeniable, but only to be explained by the telluric and solar influences.)

"There are animated bodies which exercise an action directly opposite to animal magnetism. Their presence alone is capable of destroying the effect of magnetism. This power is also a positive power." (How can there be two positive powers, one opposite to the other?)

"By means of animal magnetism, we can effect an immediate cure of the nervous diseases, and a mediate cure of all other disorders; indeed, it explains the action of the medicaments, and operates the crisis." (True, if properly explained.)

"The physician can discover by magnetism the nature of the most complicated diseases." (True, if the fact of somnambulism had been proved.)

If the French philosophers and physicians had not been blinded by the prejudices of the schools, they would have discovered amidst the errors of the theories of Mesmer some luminous truths, which would have led them to that enquiry into those fact which he covered under a magical veil. Instead, however, of examining Mesmer's system, they rejected it altogether as a nonentity; and such was the stupidity of those preachers of liberty that they turned their fury even against Mesmer's friend, Dr. D'Eslon. They deprived him, for a year, of his voice in the college of medicine, and threatened into the bargain to expel him from the fraternity if he continued to defend Mesmer's

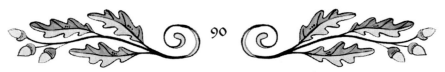

doctrine. But this brutal attempt to oppress the new discovery did not succeed. Mesmer having performed some remarkable cures, which were made public by his patients, animal magnetism was established for ever. In a short time he had realized by his cures the sum of 400,000 francs. The treatment was still practiced under a mysterious form; and the knowledge of the hidden parts of the system, namely, somnambulism, was communicated to adepts, who, after having paid a certain sum, were received into a kind of magical or medical free-masonry. The adepts formed several societies, called "Harmonies." Among the most ardent and benevolent followers of Mesmer were the Marquis of Puysegure, Caullet de Veaumorel, Petetin, and Bergasse. Magnetic societies were soon spread over France, where some still exist. The success of Mesmer daily increasing, the government of France appointed two commissions to examine his discoveries, but the commissioners being altogether prejudiced against it, gave a most partial and unsatisfactory verdict. Jussieu, the great botanist, was the only one who gave himself the trouble to examine the facts, and he was so entirely convinced, that he published his opinion in contradiction to the verdict of the commissioners. The college of physicians, in the joy of the triumph obtained, again attacked Eslon, who had opened a magnetical establishment in opposition to Mesmer. They caused his name to be erased from the list of members of the college, and obtained a royal ordonnance, by which he and his pupils were prohibited from performing magnetical cures.

These measures, instead of producing the desired effect, increased the number of the followers and defenders of the new doctrine. Mesmer became, at the same time, the object of the most superstitious idolatry, and of the most fanatical persecution. His friends, of both sexes, wore his portrait on bracelets, brooches, snuff-boxes, seals, &c; and the press teemed with works for and against Mesmerism.

In the meanwhile, the French Revolution burst forth like a roaring tempest; and Mesmer, who foresaw all the terrible consequences of the event, left France, and retired to his native land, where he remained in perfect seclusion, and continued to elaborate in silence his system, and to cultivate a little estate, "*procul negotiis, ut prisca gens mortalium.*" Here also he wrote a most interesting work, a kind of political medicine, in which he first gave birth to ideas which bear a great similarity with those advocated by modern Utopists.

Whilst Mesmer lived in retirement, insulated, as it were, from all the scientific world, the sciences were making in Germany the most astonishing progress. The spirit of philosophical enquiry had penetrated into all branches of medicine. All fact, all experiences, all theories, were put into the crucible of criticism; nothing escaped the penetrating, truth-seeking, independent genius of the Germans. How could the discovery of Mesmer remain unnoticed? How remain unnoticed, when such as Schelling, von Humboldt, Ritter, Treviranus, Walther, Hufeland, Eschenmayor, Nasse, Nees of Esenbeck, Francis Bader, Kieser, began to devote their attention to Mesmerism? This discovery, examined by the most impartial, learned, and conscientious men, divested of all jugglery and secrecy, soon assumed the character of certainty. The most talented physicians found therein one of the most efficacious remedies; the physiologists, one of the most important phenomena in neurology; the philosophers, one of the most remarkable facts explanatory of the most recondite phenomena of spiritual agency; the historian and divine, one of the most striking discoveries, unveiling the wonders and miracles, the dreams and prophecies of all nations.

Public lectures on magnetism were appointed by government in different universities. The Prussian government established an hospital for magnetic treatment, and sent the director of this

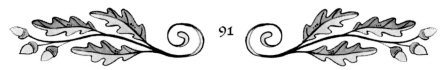

establishment to Switzerland to obtain from Mesmer all the necessary information. Professor Wolfart went to Frauenfeld to visit the great inventor, who, a few years before his death, had the satisfaction of seeing his works edited by one of the professors of the first university in the world, and his science triumphant in Berlin, Jena, Bonn, Halle, Tubingen, St. Petersburg, Copenhagen, and in several towns of France, Holland, and Sweden. Yes, even in Vienna, where the discovery was made known, where every attempt of reform is doomed to be crushed under the weight of absolute despotism,—even in Vienna, in spite of the laws and lawgivers, animal magnetism has performed, and is performing, the most wonderful cures, under the able treatment of one of the most talented and fashionable physicians, Dr. Malfatti.

And shall England be deprived of the benefit of this discovery,—be deprived, because a false spirit and mind-killing philosophy is exercising its despotic powers to the utter destruction of all scientific and social improvements?

Shall the fear of ridicule, sarcasm, and calumny, deter the lover of truth from speaking his conviction, and from sealing his conviction by acting according to the dictates of the new doctrine? Certainly not; and if all the thunders of a corrupt press, if the wrath of all the congregated professions should conspire against truth, the truth will be manifested, and proved by

THE ALPINE PHILOSOPHER.

Letter VIII

Deus mundo immersus, mundo emergitur semper.
God, immeged in nature, emerges continually from nature.

Whoever wishes to penetrate the inmost recesses of nature, must purify himself, by laying aside all envious thoughts, all prejudices, and that towering pride, which paralyzes, as it were, the nerve of the spiritual eye. God has placed nature amidst the broad daylight, as a mysterious sphinx; she speaks, and her words are the words of God; but these words are hieroglyphs for the profane. In the same way as the illiterate Indian would gaze at a printed book, unable to decipher the combinations of its letters, so the profane stands before the living letters of the Lord: "He has eyes, and cannot see; he has ears, and cannot understand." But the ever kind mother has pity upon the weakness of her children; from time to time she lifts up her veil, and the eternal life of God reveals itself in flaming letters.

When this occurs, many facts that were assumed to be true appear as errors, many systems founded upon these assumed facts sink into nothingness, and facts that were denied, because they would not agree with favourite systems, are again called back as evidence of systems, to which the revelations of nature impart an undeniable truth. But the mock philosophers, and the mock divines, to whom every new revelation is a death-blow, because they live upon the ignorance of their followers, as soon as a new beam of heavenly light irradiates the world, both unite together, to smother, if possible, the revelation of nature.

Tellurism, or Animal Magnetism, is such a light. Is it to be wondered at, if this discovery has hitherto met with powerful opposition, so powerful as to have prevented its yet being spread in this country?

Besides the difficulty which every revelation of nature has to meet with, Animal Magnetism has

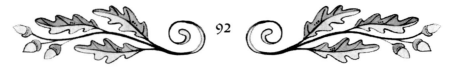

many peculiar disadvantages to contend with. The artificial mode of living counteracts in a certain degree the natural action and reaction of the elementary powers of nature. We are awake when the telluric influence calls us to sleep; when the solar power would awake us, we consume the best hours in unrefreshing sleep. Our digestion impaired by unnatural living (too high or too low); our vital powers paralyzed by poisoning passions, toils, cares, vices; the air which we breathe impregnated with impurities; even the fluid which nature prepares so carefully mixed with putrefaction; our nervous fluid, our blood, corrupted even in the womb of our mothers, by oxides and protoxides of metals, and by drastic medicines:—all these circumstances often make the patients, for a long time, restive to the influence of tellurism.

Moreover, such is the power of fashion, that men bred in colleges are afraid to lose their dignity by performing a magical operation, like that of magnetism. And if that was not the case, their interest would not allow them to attend to this mode of treatment.

The somnambulist requires often the whole attention of the physician during hours; and that for several weeks—yea, months! And in certain cases the somnambulists have the impertinence to discover the mistakes of the doctors, and the insolence to prescribe for themselves, without paying the least attention to the sayings and doings of the learned faculty!

Dr. Wienhold, in Bremen, once treated magnetically Miss R., a young lady highly gifted, but entirely unacquainted with medicine. On one occasion this lady prescribed, during somnambulism, the decoction of certain herbs, which she described most accurately, without knowing their botanical names. The herbs prescribed were not only unknown to the medical world, as possessing any antispasmodic or nervine properties, but unknown also as officinal to all compounders of domestic medicines. Still the young lady persisted in demanding the decoction. The doctor, looking at his Floras, thought that these herbs could not be found at that season of the year. Upon his making this observation, the somnambulist pointed out the very spot, about a mile and a half from town, where they would be found. The doctor, in company with *Olbers*, the great astronomer, went to the place designated, and to his great astonishment, found the herbs. He collected them, and brought them, together with other herbs, bound in bundles, and presented them to the patient whilst in magnetic sleep; Miss R. chose among the different bundles those which contained the herbs that she had required for the decoction.

The same lady, upon another occasion, prescribed for herself a mixture. The doctor fancied that the dose of crocus was too large; he went to the chemist, and ordered the mixture according to the rules of art, diminishing the dose. The mixture was given to the patient while awake; she took it without knowing that she had prescribed it, and totally ignorant of its contents. The next day, when she had fallen into magnetic sleep, she reproached the doctor for his having acted in contradiction to her prescription, and insisted upon his obeying her orders. The doctor then had the mixture made up as prescribed by the somnambulist, which, instead of injuring the patient, acted most beneficially.

These are facts, the evidence of which no one can deny. But how few of the members of the collegiate wisdom would submit themselves to have their doctrine put to the test of a *clairevoyante*!

The medical art is generally exercised as a profession; the income of the medical man depends on the amount of his business. The nervous diseases, and all the various evils which depend on those numerous complicated disorders of the vegetative system, hysterics, hypochondriacism, catalepsy, epilepsy, nervous lameness, paralysis, and all that is comprehended under the name of female complaints, offer the richest harvest to the doctor, practitioner, and chemist.

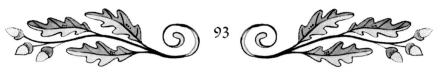

It is certain that the medical art knows nothing about these complaints. The greatest men of all ages have confessed their ignorance about these important topics. Hahneman, the author of the Homœopathic System, and his followers, have proved that the usual mode of treatment in those diseases, instead of being beneficial, is highly mischievous.

To convince our readers of the ignorance of the physician in the cure of these complaints, we need only point out that each doctor treats them in a different way; indeed, that each doctor avowedly changes the treatment of these disorders in the same individual, without any other reason but the failure of his experiments. Open the books of the physicians of all countries, observe their prescriptions, and you will find that all that the three can produce have been alternately tried to subdue these complaints.

Whilst the pupils of Hamilton and Abernethy, imagining that all these diseases depend on a disorder of the stomach, lavish the cathartics to their patients; the pupils of Brown and Roeschlaub, alternatively with these, have recourse to stimulants or contra-stimulants; the disciples of Marcus, Tommasini, Rasori, and Broussais, on the contrary, attack the same diseases with more or less sanguinary means, some covering the sufferers with leeches, others bleeding them almost to death. The empirics have extolled, by turns, the efficacy of opium, belladonna, camphor, valerian, Peruvian bark, stramonium, and veratrum; others recommend crocus, serpentaria, angustura, angelica; whilst others reckon among their favourite remedies, moschus, castoreum, oleum cajeputi, oleum animale dippel, &c. Some praise the alkalis; others, the acids. The Iatrochemists, who think of finding the safest remedies in the metallic and elementary combinations, have been prodigal with oxides and protoxides, sulphates and bisulphates, carbons, and carburets of mercury, lead, zinc, bismuth, copper, iron, barytes, and arsenic; blisters, electricity, galvanism, baths, artificial issues, moxa, and hot iron. Indeed, we know of a renowned professor and physician, who almost every year had submitted his patients to a wholesale treatment of some of these remedies. We know that he for a whole year had mercuried them; the next year they were ironed; afterwards zinced; then silvered. After a while the antiphlogistic (sanguinary) system became his favourite one; and now the salts and sulphates of the narcotics, strychnia, veratrina, and such like, are the enchanted arms by which he assails diseases.

It is evident that this contradiction among the learned, these experiments among the quacks, show plainly to every one, whose organs of perception and judgment are not impaired, that the nervous diseases, and all the complicated disorders of the vegetative system, are a god-send for those who, in playing at blind-man's-buff with nature, reap a large harvest from the pockets of the credulous and ignorant. Their modes of treatment, instead of removing, complicate the diseases more and more. The use of drastics injures the powers of digestion; the use of narcotics paralyses the nerves; the antiphlogistic method destroys the vital power of reproduction; and all the mineral preparations, supposing they succeed in removing for a while the most tormenting symptoms of the disease, do not remove the cause of the disease, which, Proteus-like, breaks forth in new forms and shapes.

How many, even of the wealthiest of society, are thus continually afflicted, exchanging disorder for disorder! How many are deprived, in their most blooming age, of the greatest gift of nature, a sound body! How many mental disorders originate and are rendered incurable by the improper use of those remedies, which the learned lavish upon their patients only for the sake of concealing their own ignorance, or for gaining pelf, by practising upon the credulity of others!

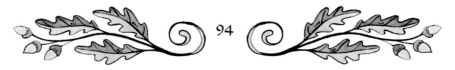

Now for those diseases for which the medical art has no compass to steer by; for the nervous diseases under all forms, as well as for the diseases of the vegetative system, and particularly for female complaints, Tellurism, or Animal Magnetism, is a specific remedy. Such diseases are convulsions, fits, hysterics, epilepsy, catalepsy, affections of the eyes and ears, general and partial nervous lameness, all sorts of congestions and hæmorrhages, disorders of menstruations, disorders of digestion, nervous headaches, tic-douloreux, incipient dropsy, all incipient cutaneous diseases, pains in the limbs, scrofula, nervous debility, and nervous decline; all these disorders, if the vital power has not been destroyed by the abuse of medicines, can be cured radically by Tellurism.

In these disorders, when the vital power has not been too much impaired, the cure is operated by Animal Magnetism alone, without the aid of any other remedy. If these disorders are treated by Magnetism in their beginning, their cure is almost miraculous, the patient recovering his health without scarcely feeling the effects of the treatment.

If the disorder by of long standing, and complicated, the cure is effected by somnambulism, and often by remedies prescribed by the patient during magnetic sleep.

We shall now give some accounts of cures performed by magnetism. We extract the following account from the Acts of the Philosophical Society of Berlin, of the 13th of December, 1811.

Dr. Metzdorf, in Berlin, a physician, was called to a lady of eighteen years of age, who was labouring under a severe illness. She complained of continual pains in the head, fits, want of appetite; she suffered from oppression in her chest, and want of respiration; her skin was dry and hot. These symptoms were aggravated by want of rest, and a melancholy bordering on insanity. The menstruation was regular; the pulse hard and feverish; her bowels constipated. After having tried cathartics and bitters, tonics and balsamics; after having endeavoured by all means to promote perspiration; in short, after having acted according to all the rules prescribed by the schools, the doctor at last, in despair, resolved to try the power of Animal Magnetism. He had never tried it before, and had but little faith in its efficacy. The young lady was altogether an unbeliever.

The trial began the 29th of October, at twelve o'clock in the morning, in the presence of the mother and the sisters of the patient. After five minutes' manipulation, she found the pains diminishing; she felt heaviness in her eyes. The operation lasted ten minutes. After the departure of the doctor, she laid herself on the sofa, and slept an hour. She awoke with less pains than usual. During the night she had for the first time good rest since her illness. The next day the manipulation lasted for ten minutes, after which she fell asleep, and slept for two hours. The pains decreased, and she passed a good night.

On the third day, after having been manipulated at the usual hour for about ten minutes, she fell asleep, and slept *four* hours. She awoke with but little headache, and with good appetite; her bowels had become regular.

The first of November the same favourable results from the manipulation, with the addition of a gentle perspiration.

The doctor was prevented for two days running from attending his patient; the consequences were, convulsions, melancholy, dreadful headache, loss of appetite, and costiveness.

The fifth of November, at seven o'clock in the evening, the treatment was resumed. She complained of heaviness in the arms during the manipulation. Excellent night's rest.

On the sixth the headache had diminished. The treatment was continued as before. After five minutes' manipulation, she fell asleep, and slept one hour and a half, which was followed by

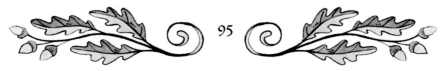

abundant perspiration. Her appetite was restored, and costiveness removed.

Under the same treatment she continued to improve. On the eighth she was not magnetised, and slept very little, and was restless.

The ninth she awoke very weak, but got better after the magnetical operation.

The tenth the treatment was painful to the patient. She felt a contraction in the whole body; she was unable to move a single limb, or even to speak; her facial muscles were convulsed. The treatment was continued longer than usual, and all these symptoms disappeared. After the manipulation she fell asleep, and awoke in the possession of her full health. No trace of convulsions, or of headache, remained. Her melancholy had disappeared. The young lady left that very evening her sick chamber, visited some friends, and enjoyed with liveliness an impromptu dancing party given to celebrate her recovery.

The perfect cure of a disease was completed which had baffled the skill of the medical art.

Here the cure was effected by the direct influence of the magnetic treatment. This alone brought into harmony the discordant strings of her afflicted frame, by restoring digestion, perspiration, and rest; and thus removing constipation, fits, and melancholy.

Had Dr. Metzdorf, like some of the old school, continued to attack the disease by drugs and minerals, most probably the young lady would now have increased the number of the unhappy beings who are condemned to be immured in public or private mad-houses.

In a similar way, many of the most eminent physicians in Berlin, Bremen, Dresden, Stuttgard, and Bamberg—such as Hufeland, Weinholt, Kieser, Nasse, Fischer, Nordhof, Schelling, Brandis, Marcus, and Gmelin, have cured nervous and other complicated complaints, without producing any other visible effect than the cure itself.

And is it not the same with the formation of the diseases? Do they not arise insensibly to the stage which announces to us their existence? This way of a quite insensibly acting medium, is it not in harmony with the whole system of nature?

To the witness of those men, I can boldly add my own experience. I have healed many nervous and complicated female complaints, without carrying the treatment so far as to produce somnambulism. Indeed, I think it very wrong to bring forth this phenomenon by main force. Yet, when it develops itself as it were voluntarily, then we may be sure that its results will be beneficial to the patient, and impart instruction to the philosopher.

In the next letter I shall give a most curious history of a magnetical cure performed by myself upon a lady in Chur, in Switzerland, who, in the thirty-second year of her age, and in the third month of pregnancy, was confined to bed with a flux, declining fever, fits, and swoons, and want of rest and appetite. She was perfectly cured, after having passed through the highest degrees of somnambulism.

To-day, I take leave of you, my dear Shepherd, and beg you to let your readers know, that if any of them feel inclined to try this power, they may address themselves to

THE ALPINE PHILOSOPHER.

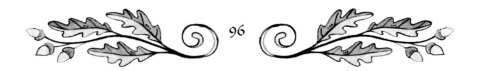

Letter IX

Anch' io son pittore!
I myself am a magician!

———

Often whilst I wandered over the Alps, when the eagle soared over my head, where the waters of the mountain rushed in torrents from the cliffs in the deep abysses; when the avalanche, with thundering fury, hurled from the ice mountain, involving in the whirl of its ravages rocks, trees, cottages, and cattle; when the clouds under my feet moved to and fro like the hosts of the Lord arrayed for battle; often in this majestic scenery I felt my heart beat louder and louder; my soul longed, as it were, to leave the heavy burden of the body, and to expand itself like an invisible gas through the blue arches of the temple of Nature. It was then, also, that my mind first meditated on the primitive laws of universal life; that life which, through the means of the two principles (bipolarity), calls forth plurality from unity, and unity from plurality, and presents the phenomena of light and gravitation, centripetal and centrifugal power, attraction and repulsion, sympathy and antipathy, good and evil, health and disease, liberty and necessity. It was then that I found, also, that all that is has a double life, an individual and a universal one; and that both forms of life are but manifestations of the one spiritual life, which is God emerged and emerging from nature. I found that his magnetic spark kindles the whole creation, and that the ashes are nothing but seeds of new combinations.

One day, 1st October, 1819, while returning from one of these excursions – it was on a beautiful autumnal evening, when the sinking sun in the Alpine regions, and particularly in the valley of Chur, presents one of the most glorious specimens of sublime scenery that I ever witnessed. I was about two miles distant from town, when I met the Rev. Mr. K., one of the principal clergymen of the synod of that canton. "I am just looking out for you," said this gentleman, "and I am glad to find you, and to meet you alone, that I may have a little conversation with you." He then took my arm, and began to relate the history of the malady of his wife, whom I knew not even by sight. After having complained how hard he had been visited by God, he finished, saying "and yet I have a hope to have her restored, if you will undertake her cure." "But how shall I cure her," replied I, "if all those consummate physicians of whom you speak have failed? You have consulted Autenrieth, Rahn, Eschenmayer, Plouquet, and many others; her present physician is a very able man; how can you have confidence in me, who am quite a stranger to you?" "I know that you have studied animal magnetism," replied the parson, "and it is in animal magnetism that I put my trust: would you be kind enough to undertake a magnetical cure?" "I must first see the patient," answered I; "secondly, I must be sure that, from the moment I undertake the treatment, all kinds of physic be banished. Either I will not venture the cure, or I will take all responsibility upon myself. Moreover, are you sure to possess the self-command not to waver if any thing should occur that, according to appearance, might seem to threaten your fondest hopes with destruction?" "I trust in God and in you," said the parson. "Well, then, under these conditions, I come immediately with you;" and so along we went; and, after a short walk, we entered the sick-room.

Mrs. K., the daughter of a clergyman in Tubingen, had suffered much in her fifteenth year, from

the difficulty of menstruation; her organization, however seemed perfect; she was tall and well-formed, endowed with a temperament in which the nervous and the sanguine appeared happily mixed. From this epoch she suffered periodical accesses of hysterical convulsions, headache, &c., for several years. All means adapted to cure this habit having failed, her parents were given to understand by the physicians that matrimony alone would restore her health. A few years after, she married the Rev. Mr. K., and the predictions of the wise men seemed at first to be realized.

Yet these predictions soon turned out to be altogether fallacious. As soon as she was in the state of pregnancy she was assailed with most terrific convulsions, and loss of blood, which ended on the third month with abortion. During five years of matrimony she had suffered four times the same torments, and her constitution was every time broken down more and more. All that medical skill could suggest had been tried, but in vain. The most honest among her advisers acknowledged that they knew no more what to do. Professor E. of Tubingen advised the magnetism, but only then when the state of pregnancy was over.

The good lady was lying on her bed, reduced almost to a skeleton; she was pregnant; a flux of blood, alternating with convulsions and vomit, had deprived her of appetite, rest, and almost of the last spark of life. Her pulse was so low, that it could be felt with difficulty. The colour of her face was grey white, her lips parched, her eyes sunk. Seeing a stranger come into the room, she was attacked immediately with spasms. I made seven calming magnetic turns, with the flat hand, from the forehead to the extremity, and she was appeased. After conversing a little with the patient, I retired with the clergyman, to whom I said that the case was very dangerous, yet not to be despaired of. I would undertake the treatment, provided I could begin immediately, and have the patient wholly under my direction; to which the Rev. Mr. K. having readily agreed, I began the treatment the same evening at eight o'clock.

My treatment was first directed to stop the loss of blood, as the most dangerous symptom. After fifteen minutes' manipulation the patient felt a little fatigue, but gave no other visible sign of being in any way affected by magnetism. My treatment consisted first in elliptical calming strokes from the forehead to the feet, at half an inch distance from the body, without resting upon the stomach or the uterinal regions; afterwards in negative strokes from the uterinal regions to the stomach. All sorts of medicines were removed. The diet I ordered was farinaceous and mucilaginous food – sago, gruel, &c.

The second day the same treatment. My simply crossing the stomach with the calming strokes, caused, after ten minutes' manipulations, a violent spasmodic asthma, which I was obliged to relieve by ventilation. I continued the operation for twenty minutes; after which she felt herself a little relieved. She had passed a more easy night, and had taken a little food without vomiting. Thus I continued for seven evenings, without any abatement of the symptoms. The seventh evening, after ten minutes' manipulation, the asthma became more violent than usual. I placed gently one hand over the plexus, and one over the forehead. Instantly the spasmodic attack cased, and a few minutes after she fell asleep, and awoke after half an hour visibly improved. She drank a bottle of magnetic water.

The following night she slept soundly, and dreamed, and spoke during her dream. Her husband, who watched her, could not comprehend her broken language. He put his hand upon her plexus, but immediately was obliged to remove it, his wife being immediately attacked with the spasms.

The next morning she awoke quite refreshed; to the astonishment of her husband and nurse the

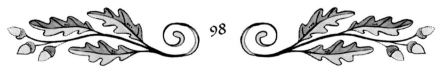

blood was stilled, and she felt herself so much better, that she could get up from her bed, and walk about in the room. On the evening of the eighth day I found the patient sitting in an easy chair; her lips were already more coloured, and her whole countenance announced more strength. On that evening she fell asleep after five minutes' manipulation. I continued, however, to operate for ten minutes longer, when she gave me to understand with a nod that it was enough.

Nothing particular occurred till the fourteenth evening. In the interval, however, her health had improved. On that evening, scarcely had I finished the third general palmar manipulation, when her eyes began to roll convulsively; her eyelids to shut and to open with great quickness; after which she gave a loud deep sigh, and fell into a high degree of somnambulism. I continued the operation for ten minutes; I observed that she tried to utter some words, but was unable to do so on account of a spasm in her tongue. I magnetized her throat and chin, and after a while she was able to say "Water, water!" I gave her a glass of magnetized water, which she drank with greediness, and exclaimed, "Oh, that is good and strengthening!" She made me signs to continue the strokes over her chest, and over the extremities. After a while she said "It is enough." I was fixing her with my eyes, and with the most concentrated will, to make her speak. She continued silent for some minutes, then she addressed me: "Do not force me to speak this evening; I am too weak. It is yet too dark around me, and in me. I see nothing but a feeble gas around you; also the water shines a little. I shall sleep thirty-three minutes longer; but tomorrow I shall see clearer."

But it was on the 20th day that the somnambulist gave the first opportunity to observe the power of the telluric life in some of its most remarkable features. On this evening she foretold that her cure would be accomplished on the 28th of December, but that she ought to be magnetized a month longer, in order to give strength to her foetus. She was asked whether she would have a lucky child-bed. "To be sure," answered she; "you magnetize me, I magnetize the dear little creature, and we shall both do very well." "Can you tell me whether it is a boy or a girl?" "A boy; a nice health boy! Now I am thankful to you that you have preserved his life, and my life too."

After a moment's silence she showed great sorrow in her face, and then exclaimed, "My child will live, though nobody ever dreamt I should recover; but Mrs. B. will soon have to bewail the death of her baby, though he looks the picture of health." She spoke that in the presence of some gentlemen and ladies. Both events took place literally as foretold.

From this time the somnambulism developed itself clearer and clearer. One evening she was asked whether she would see a patient, and prescribe for him. "I will do what I can, though I know nothing of physic." The patient was a gentleman aged twenty-three, who was given up as incurable by several physicians. His disease had been named first a nervous, then a tracheal decline. The young gentleman was introduced to her; she desired me to take his hand, and place it upon her stomach. After five minutes' silence: "Oh, the doctors!" exclaimed she. "Behold another victim of their absurdities! This young man suffers from worms; I see them moving in the slime of his bowels; and his physicians have ordered him blisters. Have you not a blister now over your chest? The patient answered in the affirmative. "Go home and put it away, and have it dressed, and have all phials thrown into the dust-hole."

A gentleman begged me to ask what kind of worms afflicted the poor young man. "I do not know their names; but I see them. Here (she pointed to the higher bowels) I see the one kind, some half a foot long; I see them curling. Here (she pointed to the lower bowels) are the small ones; small and thin, but very lively."

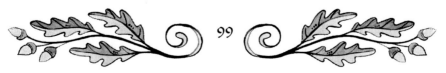

"How do you see that?" asked I. "I do not know how, but I know that it is so."

"What shall he take to remove them?" urged I. "You are a physician, and you know it yourself; but I will think of something." She afterwards prescribed a powder composed of seeds, some bitter aromatic bark, and sulphate of iron. She did not know how to name the seeds nor the bark; but she would be able to choose the right ones, if presented to her.

I sent to a friend of mine, an apothecary, to send me several samples of seeds and aromatic barks. He sent the seeds of mustard, santonicum, sabadilla, cumin, and anebtic; and the Peruvian bark, cascarilla, sassafras, Angustura vera, Angustura spuris, and horse-chestnut. The seeds were first presented to her; she put each of them upon her plexus, and chose semen veratri sabadil. I asked whether she knew this seed before, or its virtue? She denied it. Among the barks she chose the Angustura vera, which she likewise never had known before.

I asked whether the other bark, the Angustura spuria would do the same, and she answered no; it would be injurious. I put then the Peruvian bark into her hands and repeated the same question. She began to smile. "That bark I know too well; and the gentleman knows it also; we both have had enough of it."

"How much shall the patient take of these powders?" "I will show it to him tomorrow evening. I begin to be fatigued."

This fact, of which several persons were witnesses, is one of the most decisive in the matter of somnambulism. The young man took off his blister, threw all the physic into the dust-hole, and after having taken two of the powders, the fact proved the justness of the somnambulist's clear sight. By continuing this method and the use of a bitter wine, which she on another occasion recommended, the young man was completely recovered.

It was, however, with the greatest difficulty that I could bring her to prescribe any thing for herself. Magnetism, and magnetic water, and magnetic food, was all that she could prescribe for herself. Her health improved rapidly, and her clairvoyance brought daily new customers before her, not only to seek physical, but in some cases also moral advice.

A lady, Mrs. B., the wife of a colonel in the Swiss service in France, had for a long time heard nothing of her husband. She had written to some other friends, but by some chance or other she had been deprived of an answer. The poor lady was fretting, and to have some consolation she requested me to allow her to put a question to the somnambulist. I never allowed any one to annoy her, unless having her permission. At that epoch, there was no need to magnetise her to bring her into the crisis. My will had then such an influence, that I could bring her to sleep whilst walking down the street to visit her. So I did that evening on which I wished to introduce the wife of the colonel. I found my patient asleep when I entered the room. Two friends were sitting by her side; one, the first magistrate of the town, the other the husband of the lady whose child's death she foretold.

When I approached her, and asked whether the lady in question might be sent for; she replied, "it is quite superfluous, my friend; her husband is on the road to her, and will be here at nine o'clock; but send to her, and let her know, because otherwise, her nerves might suffer too much." One of the gentlemen went to the lady with the news, and remained there waiting for the result. By the stroke of nine, a postchaise was before the door with the beloved husband.

These are facts; and similar facts have occurred at the same time in Berlin, Paris, Stuttgard, Carlsruhe, and St. Petersburgh. The somnambulists, in all these cases, were respectable persons,

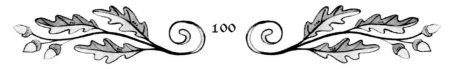

broken down with disease, and who had no other aim, no other end, but to be cured; and where the physician and philosopher had no other object in view but the mediate one of relieving the disease, and the more general one of forwarding the science.

On the evening in which the somnambulist had so clear a view of that which was passing at a distance, she also gave the most clear examen of her inward structure, to the satisfaction of a skeptical anatomist, who went away with the idea that the lady must have acquired this knowledge in her youth, from reading anatomical books, and overhearing the conversations of medical professors. But the good lady, when awake, knew not even the distinction between nerve and muscle, or vein and artery; she had received a very excellent, religious, moral, and liberal education; but had been kept entirely from the study of the structure of the human body.

After having described the healthy state of her inside, she broke out in bitter complaints against the physicians who had destroyed her vigour by the abuse of medicines. "I shall now get well," said she; "but I have here an organic disease which affects my nerves." She showed me then a kind of knot, which was formed by a bundle of crural nerves. "This knot ought to be cured, but it can never be entirely removed: it is of too long standing; the only remedy for softening it is the juice of the common onion, which must be obtained in the following way." Here she described the method of extracting or decocting the juice most minutely; and I must observe that, during the day, she had the greatest horror at the sight of onions, and would absolutely not use that which she had prescribed for herself during the somnambulism, so that we were obliged to anoint her during the crisis.

The somnambulism ceased at the end of the third month. I magnetized her the whole month following, thirty minutes each time. The sleep that followed the manipulation decreased from day to day. The last week the magnetism had lost, apparently, all power over her. But her cure was so full and perfect, that she astonished every one who had known her before. She looked strong and healthy; appetite, rest, every function were restored. At the end of nine months she gave birth to a healthy, vigorous boy.

This lady is the first, but not the only patient, whom I restored to health by somnambulism. I had several of them, more or less clear-sighted. I have chosen this case because of the quality of the disease, the circumstances which accompanied it, and the felicity of the result, seem to go as near to the point as any of those reported by the magnetists of other countries.

I cannot help mentioning a laughable occurrence which took place on this occasion. Two female attendants of the patient, peeping through the key-holes whilst I was magnetizing her mistress, saw me moving my hands in a strange way, whilst her master, with a book in his hand, stood near her bed, thought we performed some enchantment. They were so frightened at it, that both were seized with spasms and other complaints, which made the poor females fancy that they were bewitched; in consequence of which they went and accused me formally before the chief ecclesiastical authority of the canton, although he did all he possibly could to persuade them of their folly. Seeing the impossibility of checking my magic, they both left the service of Mrs. K., and spread abroad the tale that I had transplanted the disease of their mistress to them.

Behold the origin of the magical reputation of THE ALPINE PHILOSOPHER.

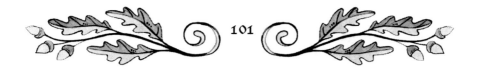

Letter X

Wie sich der Sonne Scheinbild, in dem Dunst-kreis
Malt, ehe sie kömmt, so schreiten auch den grossen
Geschicken ihre Geister schon vorans;
Une, in dem Heute wandelt schon der Morgen. — Schiller.

As the image of the sun paints itself on the mist, before his rising, thus foreboding spirits precede great events; because the future is already moving in the present.

———

The contents of the last letter may appear strange to those who, lost in the turmoil of daily business, have not had either wish or leisure to devote their attention to some phenomena of nature, which bear the strongest analogy to those of artificial somnambulism.

These phenomena are the dreams, the visions of the prophets, natural somnambulism, the last moments of dying persons, and several forms of fancies and reveries of persons afflicted with nervous diseases, fevers, and mental derangements; beside which many of the instinctive actions of insects, birds, fishes, and other animals. Indeed, the whole of nature, even that part which the scientific world most ignorantly call dead, or inorganic nature—stones, minerals, the gases; see, feel love, hate, and perform many actions, which the hackneyed systems of philosophy and physiology attribute exclusively to animals possessed of the five organs of sensation. Truly, each element is in a state of somnambulism, and each has a soul and a language to express its thoughts.

The explanation of this analogy, however, will form the subject of several letters. To-day I shall continue the practical and medical part of the science of tellurism. Our readers must understand, what I cannot often enough repeat, that somnambulism is but one of the visible effects of the telluric treatment; an effect that seldom presents itself in the purity described in my former narration, and which, in its development, presents as many forms and varieties as may be found in the varieties of the human race.

Somnambulism is not necessary to the happy results of tellurism; the most wonderful cures are generally performed without it. A conscientious telluric physician will never force his patient into this state; and when it occurs spontaneously, he will watch with all his power to prevent strangers from crowding around his clear-seeing somnambulist. The want of these precautions has done more harm to the science than all the declamations and calumnies of prejudiced scribblers, and fanatic or interested antagonists.

I know a gentleman in France, who, upon his wife's being thrown into somnambulism, had opened his house as a kind of fortune-telling institution. The visitors paid fees; and this business succeeded so well, that the house was crowded every day. The consequence was, that the somnambulist was so oppressed with questions, that she awoke from the state of somnambulism in a state of insanity.

Tellurism is the most powerful agency in nature; it is a blessing in the hands of the philosopher, but a curse in the hands of the ignorant and of the empiric. I told my readers that there are many forms under which somnambulism appears; and to prove my assertion by facts, I shall relate the history of another magnetical cure, performed in the same town as the last.

My patient was a single lady, the daughter of a magistrate (Mr. J.), aged twenty-eight. Four years

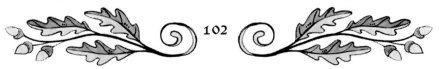

before she had recourse to tellurism she had caught cold in returning one night from a ball on an open sledge. From that period her menstruation was almost entirely suppressed; and the consequences of this suppression were fits, tic douloureux, head-ache, and occasionally mental derangement. Nothing was spared by her family in order to restore her health. She consulted the most renowned physicians at home and abroad; she was bled, leeched, and cupped; cathartics, tonics, aromatics, the martials, were lavished upon her in draughts, pills, powders, and electuaries; the natural baths of Pfeffers, of Baden, of Schinguadi, were resorted to. She drank the mineral waters of Seltzer and Pyrmont. She quitted the valley of Chur for the mountains of Engadin in vain. She gave up all in despair.

Notwithstanding all the injurious treatment which Miss J. had endured, her appearance, at first sight, was that of a person in full health; yet her nights were restless, her look wild and erratic, her head hot, her hands and feet cold as ice. Head-aches and nervous fits afflicted her; and every month, towards the full moon, a severe attack of mental derangement.

I began the treatment of her on the 1st of September, 1821. For forty days I magnetised her regularly every morning, at eleven. The manipulation lasted thirty minutes; yet during this whole period not a visible sign of action or reaction was to be observed. The fortieth day, however, scarcely had I finished the third stroke, when she fell on a sudden asleep, and so fast asleep, that when I finished the operation I left her to the care of her eldest sister, and found her still asleep two hours after.

The next day a similar occurrence. The third day the sleep had already passed into somnambulism.

In this state she lost the use of her arms and legs, yea, the whole body presented the appearance of catalepsy, with the exception of her head. The countenance presented again the traces of serene beauty. Her voice was more sonorous, her language more choice, than usual. I asked her whether she saw any thing in the room, and she answered she saw every thing in a beautiful light. I caused her eyes to be bound with a double silk shawl, and repeated my question. "I see every thing," answered she. I made then several trials, presenting different objects to her plexus, and she distinguished the most minute objects and movements. Colours she distinguished into light and dark. "In three weeks," said she, " I shall be well; but before that time I shall suffer much. The magnetism is now concentrated in me; I am like a cloud full of electricity. This evening, at seven o'clock, I shall have a violent nervous attack. You must be with me, and give me plenty of water; three bottles at least. I must have every day seven bottles of water, and the last week nine bottles every day, but well magnetised. To-morrow I shall see more clearly; but will have no sick people around me. I cannot see their diseases, and it would pain me to see their disappointment." In the evening she had gone to see a friend, where I went to watch her. Scarcely had the clock struck seven, than she uttered a shriek, and fell to the ground. She lay there as if dead for some minutes, then started up, and whilst I was approaching her to take her by the hand, I received a shock similar to that of a torpedo, and my arm felt the pain of it for several days. She threw herself, half exhausted, upon a sofa. I began then to offer her some water, and in less than an hour and a half she drank the three bottles. She did all this in a kind of half-sleep.

The clear sight increased daily. The seventh day she could distinguish every colour. Red caused convulsions; violet pleased her very much. On that day I discovered by accident the immense power of sympathy which existed between her and me. On entering her room I felt a slight attack of the

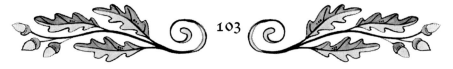

tooth-ache. After having performed a few manipulations, she complained also of tooth-ache. I made then the following experiments:—after having bound her eyes, I put some salt in my mouth; she immediately said, "O, how nasty!" I then masticated some pepper, and she became uneasy, and said, "O fie; that burns my palate." I pinched violently my finger, she exclaimed, "Be not so childish to torment me; I have some important matters to communicate to you." Whilst she was thus addressing me, Mr. R. came into the room; she, however, continued: "The rector has spoken the moat horrible things of you. He said you had made a compact with the Devil, and endeavoured to persuade a member of the Government to have you sent away."

"Pray," said the gentleman who had just entered the room, "at what hour, and in what place did the rector hold this conversation?" I repeated to her this question. "Twenty minutes ago, in the room of the castle, which has a lobby. Both he and the gentleman were looking towards the town," answered the lady.

I observed that the gentleman who had put these questions betrayed great uneasiness, and guessing that he might perhaps be the person whom the rector had endeavoured to bias against me, "Miss," said I, "did you recognize the member of government?" "To be sure I did – it was L. R." "By my honour," said the Governor, "it is all true that Miss J. has said; but I must confess to you, also, that if my principles were less philosophical, I might be inclined to find in this very circumstance a justification of the rector's opinions."

The thirteenth day Miss J. repeated her prediction, that in a week her disease would be at an end, the next day the menstruation would be restored; but the whole week she had much to endure, particularly the last three days. Upon my enquiry what she would have to endure, she replied, "I shall be like a dead body, without eating; you must be with me, but must not speak a word to me; only my sister, my brother, you, and my sister-in-law, must enter the room."

And all happened as she had said. The next day, and the three following days, she had several nervous attacks ; indeed, sometimes she was in a state of madness. The fifth day she lay stretched in her bed, dressed, in a state of total immobility. Every one in the house thought her lost. Some of her relations were already threatening the Alpine Philosopher with legal proceedings. He, full of confidence, watched, alternately with the brother and sister, his patient. The seventh day, at seven o'clock in the evening, a kind of phosphorescent light, or electrical vapour, darted from the fair sufferer. The two attending ladies fell in hysteric fits. Miss J. rose from the bed, and sunk in her brother's arms. Thus she recovered her health, which she enjoyed for many years.

Behold a somnambulist—a real somnambulist! and yet how different from that mentioned in my former letter! And what makes the difference more surprising is, that Miss J., in her ordinary walk of life, was a real female doctor. She had read books of medicine; she knew botany; and was continually making up family nostrums, to distribute among the poor. Yet in her somnambulism she would have nothing to do with the sick!

But for to-day I must leave the somnambulists at rest, and turn myself to my readers, many of whom have already honoured the Alpine Philosopher with their enquiries. Some have enquired how the operation is to be performed; whether with a particular instrument; or with the hand only? whether upon the whole body, or upon some part only? whether when dressed, or otherwise? Others have also desired to know whether tellurism proscribes all sorts of medicines, or not; and whether there be any sign to know whether the cure be accomplished.

The operation is generally performed with the hands only, which are moved, according to the

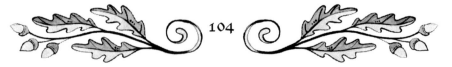

rules of tellurism, in particular directions, from the head to the extremities, resting now and then on the different plexus, or, in case of local disease, on the affected part. The manipulations are of two kinds, positive and negative – exciting and calming; some more or less so.

The tellurist is directed therein by the nature of the disease, and by the symptoms, which manifest themselves in many forms. Many of these movements are founded upon physiological principles; others have been discovered by somnambulists: and a few are merely traditional. The principle, however, that directs the whole is the law of bipolarity, which employs the positive agencies to call forth the telluric life. Even here, as in every other science, all depends on the talents, genius, good-will, perseverance, presence of mind, and discrimination of the professor.

It is sometimes necessary to strengthen or to modify the manipulations with the aid of rooms properly fitted up with music, perfumes, flowers, plants, telluric baths, &c.

One of the most powerful auxiliaries is the baquet, or telluric battery. The baquets are vessels variously constructed, filled with different metals and magnetised water, with conductors, and other arrangements. Mesmer was the first to introduce a baquet; but, in his time natural philosophy was in its infancy; the discoveries of Volta, Galvani, Ritter, Davy, Berzelius, being all posterior to his invention, his baquet was very imperfect.

Dr. Wolfart, in Berlin, has improved upon the plan of his master, and Professor Kieser, in Jena, has improved upon that of Wolfart. The Alpine Philosopher, turning to the advantage of the science the recent discoveries of Faraday, has invented a new baquet, which must excel the baquets of Wolfart and Kieser. The batteries are of the greatest use, both to prepare for the human manipulation, and to perfect the cure of those local diseases which require more time than a tellurist can devote to his patients; they are also useful in cases of any accident that might befall the tellurist.

The treatment itself is not alarming, and possesses nothing contrary to decency. If the patient is confined, the manipulation is made over the bed-clothes, otherwise he may be seated in his usual dress. One thing, however, must be observed by the ladies, namely, to lay aside their stays whilst they undergo their treatment. This invention of a corrupted taste, this Procrustes'-bed of fashion, we shall have an opportunity of exposing upon some future occasion.

Tellurism, being founded on Nature, does not proscribe the use of medicine altogether; it proscribes only its abuses, and it demands from its patients to abstain from allowing any anti-telluric doctor to interfere with the cure.

Sometimes a proper course of medicine and diet is necessary to prepare for the magnetic treatment; sometimes a bitter medicine is required to assist its operation. In certain cases a little physic is required to make the cure perfect; but the quality and quantity of the medicine presented by the tellurist differ as much from those used by the iatrochemist as Nature differs from corrupted art.

Without following exactly the system of Hahnemann, the practice of the tellurist is, in some respects, similar to his. Simple, pure drugs, mostly taken from the vegetable kingdom, rather intended to develop than to repress the symptoms of the disease, small but repeated doses, and a regimen always strictly suited to the individuality of the patient, are the rules followed by the tellurist in his medical department.

In regard to the time in which the treatment is to be left off, the tellurist has a scientific criterion, which in most cases is infallible, namely, the ceasing of the visible effects of the treatment. It is mainly a peculiarity of tellurism, that, after the cure is finished, the effects produced upon the patient during the cure, such as drowsiness, sleep, convulsive movements of the eyelids, disappear gradually

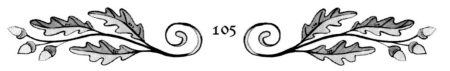

in geometrical progression, as soon as the cure is finished.

Having thus answered the general questions, I beg to inform my readers that, if any of them desire to have private consultations, they will find the tellurist at home every day from one till two p. m., at 36, Castle-street-East, Oxford-market, where letters (post paid) may be addressed.

THE ALPINE PHILOSOPHER.

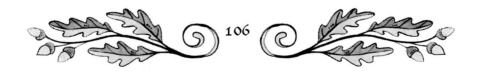

Submission Guidelines

Trilithon is an annual journal published each Alban Hefin (Summer Solstice) by the Ancient Order of Druids in America (AODA). We accept articles on the many practices of druid spirituality, specifically as those practices relate to the Druid Revival tradition. While this allows for a wide range of topics encompassing Druidry within the AODA today, we are not interested in articles criticizing anyone's vision or practice of Druidry or those that pursue a Reconstructionist or ethically exclusive agenda. For more information on Druidry within the AODA and Druid Revival tradition, we suggest reading the AODA's FAQ page or the *Druidry Handbook* by John Michael Greer.

If you are unsure if an article idea you have will fit our journal, please email our editor at trilithon@aoda.org with a query.

Length and contact information

Article submissions of up to 8,000 words are accepted; longer articles that can be divided into several parts may also be an option. When submitting your article, at the end of the manuscript itself, please also include a brief biography (up to 100 words about who you are and your path), your real name, your contact information, and then the name you prefer to appear with your article.

Originality

All submissions must be your original work and should not be under consideration at any other publication. If you collaborate with others on the piece, they must also give permission to submit the work.

References

If you are using someone else's words or ideas in your manuscript, you need to clearly cite that reference both in the text and in a references section. If you are discussing material with a long history, please refer back to the original sources when possible. All references should be in APA (American Psychological Association) format.

Use of Language

Although the AODA is based in the United States of America, we have members worldwide. We ask that articles be written in plain, non-idiomatic, English. If you are using terminology that is not well known, please define your term the first time you use it. If you are choosing an alternative spelling or capitalization in a purposeful manner, please let the editors know at the time of your submission.

Graphics

Graphics/artwork that accompanies article submissions must be included at the time of the submission and must be of high resolution (minimum of 300 dpi) and in grayscale or black and white. Artwork can be submitted as a .psd, .bmp, or .jpg file.

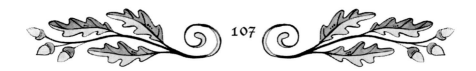

How to Submit

The article deadline for articles is February 1st for the upcoming Summer Solstice issue, although we are happy to accept articles well before that deadline. Please submit articles in .doc, .docx, or .rtf format to trilithon@aoda.org. After you have submitted your work, you can expect a response on the status of your article within three weeks' time.

Editorial Policy

If your article requires revision before publishing, our editors will contact you and provide suggestions for revision. *Trilithon* reserves the right to edit your work for publication, which may include for clarity, grammatical correctness, or conciseness.

Copyright Policy

By submitting your work to *Trilithon* you are giving non-exclusive print and digital rights for the Ancient Order of Druids in America to publish your article (or portions thereof) in *Trilithon* or on its website.

Publication Schedule

Trilithon is published yearly on Alban Hefin, the Summer Solstice. Articles for the yearly publication are due by February 1st. If you have been asked to make a revision to your article, it will be due by March 15th. Authors are free to submit anytime in the year; if your article is accepted, it will be held until our next yearly publication.

Questions and Submissions

Questions and submissions can be directed to:

Dana Lynn Driscoll
Chief Editor, *Trilithon*
trilithon@aoda.org

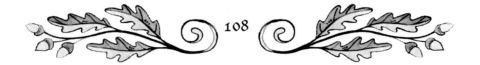

CPSIA information can be obtained at www.ICGtesting.com
Printed in the USA
LVOW09s1950220415

435657LV00007B/476/P

9 780692 211564